FUNDAMENTALS OF
RECORDKEEPING AND
FINANCE FOR THE
SMALL BUSINESS

FUNDAMENTALS OF RECORDKEEPING AND FINANCE FOR THE SMALL BUSINESS

Robert C. Ragan, CPA

Jack Zwick, Ph.D.

Introduction by Donald M. Dible

Copyright 1978 by The Entrepreneur Press

All rights reserved.

Printed in the United States of America

Published in 1978 by
The Entrepreneur Press
468 Robert Road
Vacaville, CA 95688

INTRODUCTION

It's April 14, and a small business owner makes his way to his accountant's office. With him, he has a shoe box full of receipts, invoices, and assorted scraps of paper. "I need a tax return tomorrow. I tried doing it myself, but got bogged down. Can you help me?"

While this example is sad, it's typical. Just ask any accountant if you don't believe me. An enormous number of small business owners see recordkeeping as a government-imposed requirement created so the boogeymen from the Internal Revenue Service can bleed you dry.

Frankly, I consider the recordkeeping requirements of taxation to be one of the few good things resulting from government regulation of business. If it were not for this annual reporting requirement, many business owners would never know whether they were making a profit. And, obviously, that's important.

Now, let's assume you are making a profit--or will be soon. That's not enough! To succeed in most businesses, you must grow. This takes money. Sometimes, your invested capital--plus the profits you plow back into the business--are not enough to enable you to grow as rapidly as possible. Unless you make provision for additional money, you could find yourself in deep trouble.

Strange as it may seem, there are times when too much success can be fatal. If you run out of the cash necessary to pay your suppliers and lenders in a timely fashion, they may force you into bankruptcy in order to collect. Not everyone has the patience of Job!

Recognizing how important a knowledge of recordkeeping and finance is to small business success, the writings of two eminently qualified business experts have been selected for inclusion in this book. We at The Entrepreneur Press sincerely hope you find it helpful.

Donald M. Dible
Vacaville, California

TABLE OF CONTENTS

INTRODUCTION
Donald M. Dible

FUNDAMENTALS OF RECORDKEEPING
FOR THE SMALL BUSINESS
Robert C. Ragan, CPA

FUNDAMENTALS OF FINANCE
FOR THE SMALL BUSINESS
Jack Zwick, Ph. D.

Fundamentals of Recordkeeping for the Small Business

Robert C. Ragan, CPA

Contents

Part 1. The Why, What, and How of Records

Records—For the Government or for Yourself?...... 3
Building Materials for Your Recordkeeping System.. 4
Methods and Equipment........................ 8

Part 2. The Money Comes In—and Goes Out

The Change and Petty Cash Fund................ 13
The Daily Summary of Sales and Cash Receipts.... 15
Writing the Checks............................ 19

Part 3. Lining Up the Records

The Sales and Cash Receipts Journal.............. 25
The Cash Disbursements, Purchases, and Expense
Journal.................................... 28

Part 4. Getting Set for Monthly Financial Statements

Reconciling Your Bank Statement................ 37
Recording Accounts Payable.................... 40
Merchandise Inventories....................... 42

Part 5. The Score—Win or Lose, and How Much?

The Profit-and-Loss Statement.................. 49
Departmental Operating Records................ 54

Part 6. The Shape You're In

The General Ledger and the Balance Sheet........ 63
Steps To Be Taken at the End of the Year......... 69

Part 7. The Absentee Asset: Accounts Receivable

Recording Accounts Receivable 75
Aging Your Accounts Receivable................. 81
Accounting for Bad Debts...................... 83

xi

Part 8. Some Special Cash Receipts Situations

Return Sales and Refunds........................ 87
Making Purchases from Cash Receipts............. 89
Cashing Customers' Checks....................... 90
Redeeming Coupons............................. 94

Part 9. Depreciation and Disposal of Plant Assets

Computing Depreciation of Property and Equipment. 99
Recording the Purchase and Depreciation of Plant
Assets.. 102
Recording the Sale, Trade-in, or Junking of Plant
Assets.. 107

Part 10. Here They Come—Taxes!

Collecting and Recording Sales Taxes............. 115
Payroll Records and Payroll Taxes................ 119
Income and Self-Employment Taxes.............. 126

Exhibits

1. Table of Debit and Credit Entries........................ 7
2. Petty-Cash Slip... 14
3. Daily Summary of Sales and Cash Receipts................ 16
4. Sales and Cash Receipts Journal......................... 26
5. Cash Disbursements, Purchases, and Expense Journal........ 30
6. Bank Reconciliation...................................... 38
7. Statement of Profit and Loss............................ 50
8. Departmental Purchases and Sales Record................. 55
9. Statement of Departmental Operations.................... 58
10. General Ledger Sheet.................................... 64
11. Chart of General Ledger Accounts........................ 66
12. Balance Sheet... 68
13. Accounts Receivable Ledger: Customer's Account........... 76
14. Accounts Receivable Ledger: Control Sheet................ 76
15. Aging of Accounts Receivable............................ 82
16. Daily Summary of Sales and Cash Receipts with Excess Checks
    Entry... 92
17. Depreciation Schedule................................... 104
18. Entries for Recording Disposal of Plant Assets............. 108
19. Daily Summary of Sales and Cash Receipts Showing Taxable
    Sales and Sales Tax................................... 118
20. Sales and Cash Receipts Journal Showing Taxable Sales and
    Sales Tax... 120
21. Employee Compensation Record......................... 122
22. Schedule C (Form 1040)—Profit or Loss from Business or Pro-
    fession... 127
23. Form 1065—U.S. Partnership Return of Income............ 128
24. Form 1120—U.S. Corporation Income Tax Return.......... 129
25. Form 3468—Computation of Investment Credit............ 131

Part 1 | The Why, What, and How of Records

Records—For the Government or for Yourself?......... 3

    Advantages of Keeping Good Records.................... 3

    The Records Are for You............................... 4

Building Materials for Your Recordkeeping System.... 4

    Assets, Liabilities, and Capital........................... 4

    The Framework for Your Records....................... 5

    The Basic Records..................................... 5

    Double-Entry Bookkeeping.............................. 6

    Debit and Credit Entries............................... 6

    The Trial Balance...................................... 7

    Financial Statements................................... 7

Methods and Equipment.............................. 8

    Variations in Methods of Keeping Records............... 8

    Cash and Accrual Accounting........................... 8

    Which Method Is Best for You?......................... 9

    The Records and Equipment You Need.................. 9

Records—For the Government Or for Yourself?

Why keep records?

If you are a typical small businessman, your answer to this question is probably, "Because the Government (and you mean the Internal Revenue Service) requires me to!" If the question comes in the middle of a busy day, you may add a few heartfelt words about the amount of time you have to spend on records—just for the Government!

Is it "just for the Government," though? It shouldn't be. True, regulations issued in recent years, not only by the Internal Revenue Service, but also by various other governmental agencies—Federal, State, and local—have greatly increased the recordkeeping requirements of business. But the fact is that this may be a good thing for the small businessman, overburdened though he usually is. Many studies have found a close relation between inadequate records and business failures.

Advantages of Keeping Good Records

A simple, well-organized system of records, regularly kept up, can actually be a timesaver by bringing order out of disorder. Furthermore, competition is very strong in today's business arena. A small businessman needs to know almost on a day-to-day basis where his business stands profitwise, which lines of merchandise or services are the most or the least profitable, what his working-capital needs are, and many other details. He can get this information with reasonable certainty only if he has a good recordkeeping system—one that gives him all the information he needs *and no more*.

Good records can also help to safeguard your assets. Accurate records of cash transactions will disclose any shortages, so that steps can be taken to find and correct the source of trouble. Accounts-receivable records disclose any shortages in the customers' balances and also help to control bad-debt losses. Inventory shortages are somewhat harder to detect, but here, again, a good system of records makes it possible to keep the shrinkage at a minimum.

3

Still another important use of well-organized financial records is in the preparation of financial reports showing the progress and current condition of your business. Such reports can be invaluable if you need a bank loan, or if the business must be evaluated for a sale or merger.

The Records Are for You

Think of recordkeeping, then, not as a necessary nuisance imposed by governmental regulations, but as an important tool for your own use in managing your business. Take the time, or hire an accountant, to set up a recordkeeping system that is patterned after basic accounting principles but is tailormade for *your* store. Then—grumble if you must, *but use it*. Remember, it is not just a storehouse of facts for Government use; it is a source of information that can help you increase your profits if you put it to work constructively.

Building Materials for Your Recordkeeping System

The following section of this book explains briefly some of the terms that are used over and over again in any discussion of financial records. If you are impatient, you can skip it and go directly to page 8, coming back to this section if you have trouble later with some of the terms. However, you will find the rest of the book easier going if you do read this section and make sure before going on that you understand the basic ideas involved in financial recordkeeping and the terms used.

Assets, Liabilities, and Capital

Anything a business *owns* that has a money value is an *asset* of the business. Cash, merchandise, supplies, amounts owed by customers (accounts receivable), land, buildings, furniture and fixtures, delivery equipment, and so on are assets.

Anything the business *owes* is a *liability*. Liabilities might include amounts owed to suppliers (accounts payable) or to the bank (notes payable), taxes already incurred but not yet due for payment, wages earned by employees since the last payday, and other amounts due.

The difference between what the business *owns* and what it *owes* is the amount that really belongs to the owner of the business—his *equity* or *capital* (sometimes called *proprietorship*).

The Framework for Your Records

Liabilities can be thought of as creditors' rights or claims against the assets of the business, and capital as the owner's rights.   The sum of these rights to the assets, of course, will always equal the sum of the assets themselves.   In other words, the total assets always equal the total liabilities (creditors' rights) plus the capital (owner's rights), or simply—

$$\text{Assets} = \text{liabilities} + \text{capital.}$$

Let's see how two typical business transactions affect this equation. Suppose that you pay a $50 bill from a supplier.   One of your assets— cash—will be reduced by $50.   But a liability—accounts payable—will be reduced by the same amount, so the equation will still balance.

Now suppose you buy $50 worth of supplies and pay cash for them. Again, the asset cash will be reduced by $50; but in this case, the value of another asset—supplies—will be increased by $50.   So the sum of all the assets doesn't change, and the equation still holds true.

This equation is known as the *accounting equation*.   It is the framework on which you will build your financial records.

The Basic Records

The financial records of a business begin with bits and pieces of paper— sales checks, credit memos, cash-register tapes, written receipts, check stubs, petty-cash slips, bank statements, and so on.   These papers are important.   They are the bricks from which you will build your organized, permanent records.   Some sort of written record, however informal, should always be made *at the time a transaction takes place*.

The journal.   The information from these various papers is first brought together in one or more *journals*—sometimes called "books of original entry."   A journal is simply a record of the daily transactions of the business.   Each journal entry shows (1) the date of transaction, (2) a brief description of it, (3) the amount of money involved, and (4) the assets, liabilities, capital, or type of income or expense affected by the transaction.

The ledger.   To make the information recorded in the journal more usable, each item is later transferred, or *posted,* to a ledger account.   An *account* is a record of the increases and decreases in *one type* or asset, liability, capital, income, or expense. A book or file in which a number of accounts are kept together is called a *ledger*. Exhibit 11 on page 66 shows typical accounts in a general ledger. A brief study of this will help you understand some of the following examples and transactions.

Sometimes the income and expense items are posted to a profit-and-loss statement and only the net profit or loss posted to a ledger account. This method is used in the recordkeeping system described in this booklet.

A business uses as many accounts as it needs for keeping track of its operations. A small firm with few pieces of equipment, for instance, may have only one account for all its equipment. A larger business will probably need an account for each type of equipment or even, in some cases, for a single piece of equipment. A business with only one owner will need only one capital account; a partnership will need a capital account for each partner.

Double-Entry Bookkeeping

Notice that each of the transactions used to illustrate the accounting equation (p. 5) had two effects. This is true of all business transactions, since a transaction is basically an exchange of one thing for another. Double-entry bookkeeping shows this twofold effect by recording every transaction twice—as a *debit* entry in one account and as a *credit* entry in another. Either or both of the entries may be broken down into several items, but the total of the amounts entered as debits must equal the total of the amounts entered as credits.

Debit and Credit Entries

One account may have both *debit (dr.)* and *credit (cr.)* entries. Then what determines whether an entry is to be a debit or a credit? It depends on the type of account and on whether the transaction to be entered will increase or decrease the account. Exhibit 1 shows the types of entries *(debit* or *credit)* and the typical balances for each class of accounts.

Thus, as a study of exhibit 1 will show, when you pay a bill, the amount paid is entered as a *debit* to accounts payable and as a *credit* to your cash account. When you buy supplies for cash, the amount paid is entered as a *debit* to the supplies account and as a *credit* to the cash account.

Each account sheet in the ledger has a column for the date, one for a brief description of the entry. one for the posting reference, and two for dollar amounts. *Debit* entries are always put in the left-hand dollar column and *credit* entries in the right-hand column. If the debit entries in an account total more than the credit entries, the account is said to have a *debit balance*. If the credit entries total more than the debit entries, the account has a *credit balance*. The total of all the credit balances must equal the total of all the debit balances.

Exhibit 1.—Table of Debit and Credit Entries

Type of account	If the transaction will *decrease* the account, enter it as a—	If the transaction will *increase* the account, enter it as a—	Typical balance
Asset	credit	*debit*	*debit*
Liability	*debit*	credit	credit
Capital	*debit*	credit	credit
Income	*debit*	credit	credit
Expense	credit	*debit*	*debit*

The Trial Balance

To make certain that the sum of the debit balances does equal the sum of the credit balances, a *trial balance* is taken at the end of the month (or other accounting period). This is done simply by adding all debit account balances and all credit account balances. If no errors have been made, the two totals will be the same.

The trial balance ensures that any errors will be found before they are too deeply buried. It also clears the way for preparing financial statements.

Financial Statements

The journal alone would give you a complete record of all the transactions of your business—in simple chronological order. But that isn't enough. The ledger accounts are needed to organize the details from the journal into a usable form. You need to know where the business stands financially, how well it is going, and what can be done to improve it. Ledger accounts provide for this information by grouping the transactions of your business in such a way that at any time you can prepare a balance sheet and a profit-and-loss statement.

The *balance sheet* summarizes your assets, liabilities, and capital to show the condition of your business on given date—what proportion of the assets you really own. It is called a balance sheet because it shows how the two sides of the accounting equation (assets=liabilities+ capital) "balance" in your business.

The *profit-and-loss statement* summarizes the activities of the business
during the period covered. It shows the income and expenses of the
business during that period and the profit or loss that resulted.

Methods and Equipment

The type of business you are in will affect the type of records you keep
in a number of ways. Whatever system of bookkeeping you use, the
details will have to be adapted to your special needs. It is important
to have all the information you need for your own use in managing the
business and for tax purposes. At the same time, your records should
not be cluttered with details that aren't really necessary.

Variations in Methods of Keeping Records

If a housewife buys a dozen oranges for $0.79, a grocer using the
simplest method of recordkeeping merely records the fact that a $0.79
sale has been made. He doesn't care whether the sale involves a dozen
oranges or a pound of meat.

Another grocer might want to know that $0.79 worth of fresh produce
had been sold, as opposed to meats or dry groceries. Under normal
circumstances, however, he wouldn't need to know whether the $0.79
entry on his financial records represented a dozen oranges or some other
item of fresh produce.

But if an appliance dealer, for instance, sells a television set for
$419.95, he will want to record a number of facts in addition to the
amount of the sale: the brand; the model number; trade-in information,
if applicable; sales tax, if any; service contract charge if service is
included; and so on.

Thus, a grocer would not use the same bookkeeping system as an
appliance dealer. In fact, in department or general-merchandise stores
where both groceries and television sets are sold, different systems are
generally used for recording sales in the two departments.

Cash and Accrual Accounting

Bookkeeping systems differ in the basic method of recording as well
as in the amount of detail shown. For income-tax purposes, the Internal
Revenue Service recognizes two basic methods—the *cash basis* and the
accrual basis.

When books are kept on the cash basis, no income or expense is entered
in the journal or ledger until cash is actually received or paid out. When
the accrual basis is used, income from a sale or other income-producing
transaction is entered as soon as the transaction takes place, even though

the cash may not be collected until some future date. Likewise, in accrual accounting, expenses are recorded when they are incurred, even though payment may not be made until later.

Suppose, for example, that you sell $100 worth of goods on credit. If your books are kept on the accrual basis, the sale will be entered in the journal immediately. Later, when the account is paid, you will make another entry to record the payment.

If your books are kept on the cash basis, you will keep a memorandum record of each credit customer's account. A credit sale will be noted on this account but not entered in the journal until the bill is paid.

Now suppose you pay your employees every Friday, and December 31 falls on a Monday. If you use the accrual method, you will enter the amount of the wages earned between the end of the last pay period and the close of business on December 31 as a December expense, even though you pay it in January. If you keep your books on the cash basis, you will make no entry until you pay the employees on January 4.

Which Method Is Best for You?

The Internal Revenue Service allows you to use either basis of accounting—cash or accrual—provided that (1) it clearly reflects income, and (2) you use it consistently. Internal Revenue regulations state, however, that where inventories play an important part in accounting for income, the accrual method must be used in recording sales and purchases. Since this is the case in retail stores, *the bookkeeping system described in this book uses the accrual basis for purchases and sales. The cash basis is used for expenses and for income other than sales.*

The Records and Equipment You Need

The bookkeeping system described in the remaining chapters of this book is a modified double-entry system. It uses the following "books":

> *Sales and Cash Receipts Journal.*
> *Cash Disbursements,*[1] *Purchases, and Expense Journal.*
> *General Ledger* (a record of assets, liabilities, and capital).
> *Accounts Receivable Ledger.*
> *Employees' Compensation Record.*
> A business checkbook.

These books, except for the checkbook, can be looseleaf. Standard sheets can be purchased from an office-supply store. Many different types are sold, however. Study the bookkeeping system in relation to your own business before you make your choice.

In addition to the books, several forms are needed. These are the following:

---

[1] Payments you make to others, as distinguished from payments others make to you.

Daily Summary of Sales and Cash Receipts.
Monthly customers' statements.
Employees' pay slips.
Petty-cash slips.

Printed forms for all except the *Daily Summary* can be purchased at an office-supply store. The *Daily Summary* can be an inexpensive reproduction of a typewritten sheet on which you will fill in the figures.

Mechanical equipment. In almost any type of business, an *adding machine* is needed; and if you have many transactions of the same or nearly the same type, a *cash register* is also desirable. The cash register might not be required if (1) you do not have too many transactions, and (2) the transactions are varied enough so that a sales ticket or other record would have to be written out for most sales in addition to or instead of the cash-register "ring."

If a cash register is necessary for your business, care should be taken to select one that suits your needs. You will probably want a simple machine that prints on a tape the amount and one or two other details for each transaction and that gives you one or more totals at the end of the day. The most inexpensive machines give only one total of transactions, but various symbols can be produced on the register tape. These, with an adding machine, make possible a further breakdown of transactions. Usually, a cash register that produces a receipt for the customer is desirable.

Small electronic calculators which multiply and divide have become very inexpensive and you might find one of these quite useful. With a calculator you can quickly make multiplications and divisions, compute discounts and sales taxes, figure payroll taxes, compute percentages, and make many other necessary calculations. Although these calculators also add and subtract, you should not use them in place of an adding machine to add long columns of figures, since they produce no tape which can be checked for errors.

Sales checks. If you decide that you do not need a cash register, sales checks should be used to record all sales. Sales checks are a standard item carried by most suppliers of business forms. You may, however, want to have yours printed with the name, address, and telephone number of your store. The sales checks should be prenumbered and a system used that makes it necessary to account for all sales-check numbers.

In some stores, sales checks are used for charge transactions even though cash sales are recorded on a cash register. Sales checks may also be written for cash "send" sales. A record of the charge sale is needed so that the customer's account can be debited; a record of the send sale is necessary so that delivery can be made to the proper address.

Part 2 | The Money Comes In— and Goes Out

The Change and Petty-Cash Fund..................... 13

    The Change Fund....................................... 13

    Petty Cash... 13

    A Combined Change and Petty-Cash Fund............... 14

The Daily Summary of Sales and Cash Receipts........ 15

    Cash Receipts.. 15

    Cash on Hand.. 18

    Sales... 19

    Depositing the Receipts.............................. 19

Writing the Checks..................................... 19

    Your Checkbook...................................... 20

    Supporting Documents................................ 20

    Paying the Bills...................................... 20

    Reconciling Your Bank Statement...................... 21

The Change and Petty Cash Fund

The recordkeeping system described in this book assumes that *all receipts* will be deposited in the bank. A combination change and petty-cash fund is used for all cash paid out other than by check. This practice makes it easier for you to account for cash receipts and gives you much better control over your cash.

The Change Fund

In any business where cash is received in over-the-counter transactions, it is necessary to make change. A *change fund* is kept on hand for this purpose.

The amount needed for making change varies with the size and type of business, and in some cases with the days of the week. Your daily balancing and recordkeeping will be easier, however, if you set a fixed amount for your change fund, large enough to meet all ordinary needs of the business. Then, when the day's cash receipts are balanced and prepared for deposit, you will keep bills and coins totaling the fixed amount of the fund in the cash register or till for use the following day. Since you had this amount on hand before you made the day's first sale, the entire amount of the receipts for the day will still be available for deposit.

Petty Cash

To avoid having to write many checks for small amounts, it is wise to have a *petty-cash fund* (a fixed amount) from which to make small payments. Each time a payment is made from this fund, a petty-cash slip similar to the one shown as exhibit 2 should be made out. If an invoice or receipt is available, it should be attached to the petty-cash slip for filing.

The slips are kept with the petty cash. At all times, the total of the unspent petty cash and the petty-cash slips should equal the fixed amount of the petty-cash fund. When the total of the petty-cash slips approaches the fixed amount of the fund, a check is made out to "Petty Cash" for the amount of the slips, and the money from this check is used to bring the cash in the fund back to the fixed amount.

Exhibit 2.—Petty-Cash Slip

No._____	Date_____
RECEIVED OF PETTY CASH	
Amount_____	
For_____	
Charge to_____	
Approved by:	Received by:
_____	_____

The petty-cash slips should be canceled or marked in such a way as to prevent their reuse. They are then summarized (that is, the slips are grouped according to the accounts to be charged, and the charges to each account totaled) and entered in the *Cash Disbursements Journal* described in part 3 of this booklet. A good way to handle these canceled slips is to summarize them on the outside of an envelope, showing also the date, check number, and amount of the check used to restore the petty-cash fund. The slips are then filed in the envelope.

A Combined Change and Petty-Cash Fund

In some cases, the petty-cash fund is kept in a box or safe, apart from the change fund. However, the same fund can serve for both petty cash and change. For example, if you decide that you need $50 for making change and $25 for petty cash, one $75 fund can be used. Whenever, in balancing the day's operations, you see that the petty-cash slips total more than $25, you can write a "Petty Cash" check for the amount of the slips. The slips are then handled as explained in the preceding paragraph.

The Daily Summary of Sales and Cash Receipts

Whether you use a cash register or sales checks or both, every cash receipt and every charge sale must be recorded. At the close of each day's business, the actual cash on hand is counted and "balanced" against the total of the receipts recorded for the day. This is done by means of the *Daily Summary of Sales and Cash Receipts* (exhibit 3).

If you have more than one cash register, a *Daily Summary* should be prepared for each one. The individual summaries can then be combined into one overall summary for convenience in handling.

Cash Receipts

The first section of the *Daily Summary*, "Cash Receipts," records all cash taken in during the day from whatever source. This is the cash that must be accounted for over and above the amount that was in the change and petty-cash fund at the beginning of the day.

Cash sales. The total of the cash sales is found simply by reading it from the cash-register tape or, if no cash register is used, by totaling the cash-sales checks.

Collections on account. Whether or not collections on account are rung up on a cash register, you should keep an individual record of each customer making a payment. The amount to be entered on the *Daily Summary* is found by adding these receipts. If the collections are rung up on a cash register, the total is entered from the cash-register tape. The individual receipts should also be added while the summary is being prepared, however, to make certain that their total agrees with the cash register total. If the two totals do not agree, the error should be located immediately. This can be done by comparing the individual receipts with the collection-on-account items on the cash-register tape. Handling of such errors is explained in the box on page 17.

After any errors found have been corrected, the amount shown on the *Daily Summary* as "Collections on account" should agree with the total of the customers' receipts. These receipts are then put aside and held for posting to the customers' accounts in the *Accounts Receivable Ledger* as described in part 7. Adding-machine tapes or penciled sums should also be kept for use, if needed, in checking customers' account balances.

Exhibit 3

DAILY SUMMARY OF SALES AND CASH RECEIPTS

Date March 23, 19—

CASH RECEIPTS

1. Cash sales...................................... $435. 00
2. Collections on account.......................... 100. 00
3. Miscellaneous receipts [1]....................... 15. 00
4. TOTAL RECEIPTS TO BE ACCOUNTED FOR. $550. 00

CASH ON HAND

5. Cash in register or till:
   - Coins .... $ 25. 00
   - Bills.. .... 510. 00
   - Checks............................ 95. 00
   - Total cash in register or till................. $630. 00
6. Petty-cash slips................................. 14. 00
7. TOTAL CASH ACCOUNTED FOR............. $644. 00
8. Less change and petty-cash fund:
   - Petty-cash slips...................... $14. 00
   - Coins and bills...................... 86. 00
   - Change and petty-cash fund (fixed amount)... 100. 00
9. TOTAL CASH DEPOSIT..................... $544. 00
10. CASH SHORT (Item 4 less item 9 if item 4 is larger). $6. 00
11. CASH OVER (Item 9 less item 4 if item 9 is larger). ——

TOTAL SALES

12. Cash sales...................................... $435. 00
13. Charge sales (sales checks #262 to #316)........... 225. 00
14. TOTAL SALES............................... $660. 00

By JOHN DOE

---

[1] Note to appear on back of summary: "Miscellaneous receipts: Refund on merchandise $15.00."

How To Handle Errors in Recording Collections on Account

Errors in recording collections on account may be of the following types:

- Wrong amount rung up for the collection.
- Collection rung up on the wrong key (that is, as a cash sale or other transaction).
- Collection not rung up.
- No customer's receipt for a collection recorded on the cash register tape.

Errors of the first three types are easily identified and corrected on the cash-register tape and on the *Daily Summary*. Where there is no customer's receipt for a collection appearing on the cash-register tape, the error may be harder to find. A cash sale or other transaction may have been rung up as a collection on account. Or the collection may have been rung up correctly but the receipt not prepared, or prepared but lost or misplaced.

Sometimes the person who rang up the item will remember the transaction, and a correction can be made. If the collection cannot be identified, a dummy receipt should be made out showing the amount of the collection and marked "Unidentified Receipt." Further handling of these unidentified receipts will be explained in the discussion of accounts receivable.

Miscellaneous receipts. Some cash receipts cannot be classified as cash sales or collections on account. They are entered on the *Daily Summary* as "Miscellaneous receipts." These receipts might include refunds from suppliers for overpayments, advertising rebates or allowances, collections of rent from subleases or concessions, handling charges on coupons, and so on.

A sales check or other memo should be made out for each miscellaneous receipt of cash. These notations are totaled at the end of the day to give the amount entered as item 3 of the *Daily Summary*. If you have a cash register with a key for miscellaneous receipts, the daily total of that register is used. The individual memos will still be necessary, however, because the miscellaneous receipts should be itemized on the back of the *Daily Summary*. This information is needed for records that will be explained later.

Total receipts. After the totals for the various types of cash receipts have been entered (items 1, 2, and 3 of the *Daily Summary*), these totals are added to give item 4, the total receipts for the day that must be accounted for.

Cash on Hand

The second section of the *Daily Summary,* "Cash on Hand," is a count of the cash actually on hand and the cash represented by petty-cash slips.

Cash in register or till. The money in the cash register or till is counted at the close of business. Coins, bills, and checks are recorded separately and then totaled in item 5 of the *Daily Summary.*

Petty-cash slips. Petty-cash slips represent cash that has been paid out. They are therefore totaled and included (item 6) in the cash accounted for.

Total cash accounted for. After coins, bills, checks, and petty-cash slips have been entered, their total is recorded as item 7. This total will include both the day's receipts and the amount that was on hand at the beginning of the day—the change and petty-cash fund.

Change and petty-cash fund. Item 8 of the *Daily Summary* includes the petty-cash slips on hand (until they are replaced by cash as explained earlier) and enough cash to make up the fixed amount of the fund. The amount entered here for petty-cash slips is taken from item 6. The amount of the "coins and bills" is found by subtracting the total of the petty-cash slips from the fixed amount of the change and petty-cash fund.

Total cash deposit. The change and petty-cash fund is to be kept on hand for use in the next day's operations. Therefore, the amount to be deposited in the bank (item 9) will be the total cash accounted for (item 7) minus the fixed amount of the fund (item 8). Since the fixed

---

Possible Errors in Case of a Cash Shortage or Overage

If the amount to be deposited is MORE than the total receipts recorded for the day, the overage could be caused by:

- Neglecting to record or ring up a transaction.
- Recording or ringing up a transaction for too small an amount.
- Giving a customer too little change.

If the amount to be deposited is LESS than the total receipts recorded for the day, the shortage could be caused by:

- Recording or ringing up too large an amount for a transaction.
- Giving a customer too much change.
- Taking money from the cash register or till without recording it.

amount was in the change fund at the beginning of the day, the amount to be deposited should just equal the total receipts for the day (item 4). If it does not, all work done in preparing the *Daily Summary* should be carefully checked, especially corrections to the cash-register tape. If no error is found in the counting and balancing, check the day's records for errors of the types listed in the accompanying box.

Cash short or over. If the amount to be deposited and the total receipts for the day still do not agree after the day's work has been thoroughly checked, the difference is entered as "cash short" (item 10) or "cash over" (item 11). This completes the daily summary of cash receipts.

Sales

The last section of the *Daily Summary of Sales and Cash Receipts* records the total sales for the day (item 14) by adding the charge sales to the cash sales already entered as item 1 of the summary. If you want a record of sales broken down by salespersons or departments, this can also be shown here.

The total of the charge sales is found by adding all the charge-sales checks. If charge sales are rung up on a cash register (which is usually not necessary), the total of the sales checks should be compared with the cash-register total as in the case of collections on account.

Depositing the Receipts

As soon as possible after the *Daily Summary* has been completed, all cash for deposit should be taken to the bank. A duplicate deposit slip, stamped by the bank, should be kept with the *Daily Summary* as evidence that the deposit was made.

Writing the Checks

All major payments should be made by checks drawn on a bank account used only for business transactions. If your business is typical, you will have to write checks for merchandise purchases, employees' salaries, rent, utilities, petty cash, payroll taxes, and various other expenses.

Your Checkbook

Your business checkbook should be the large desk-type checkbook. Such a checkbook usually has three checks to a page and large stubs on which to write a full description of each expenditure. It may have the name and address of your business printed on each check, and the checks should be prenumbered.

As each check is written, enter on the stub the date, payee, amount, and purpose of the payment. A running balance of the amount you have in the bank is maintained by subtracting the amount of each check from the existing balance shown on the check stub.

When a check is spoiled, tear off the signature part of the check to prevent any possibility of the check's being used, write "VOID" prominently on the check and on the stub, and staple the torn check to the back of its stub. This assures you that the check has not been used in an unauthorized way.

Supporting Documents

Every check should have some sort of written document to support it— an invoice, petty-cash voucher, payroll summary, and so on. If such support is not available for some good reason, a memo should be written stating what the check is for.

Each of these supporting documents should be approved, by signature or initials, by you or someone you have authorized to do so. The signature should indicate that the goods or services have been received, that the terms and price are correct, and that no error has been made in computing the amount to be paid. It is especially important to see that cash discounts, when offered, are correctly computed and deducted.

When each check is written, the supporting document should be marked "Paid" and the date and check number shown. If the checks are prepared for your signature by an employee, you should see the supporting document before you sign the check. Make certain that it is marked in a way to prevent its being paid a second time. After payment has been made, this supporting material should be filed in a paid-bills file in alphabetical order by payee.

Paying the Bills

Bills are usually paid once a month unless there are special discount terms or special arrangements with suppliers for daily or weekly settlement. Most vendors send monthly statements, often in addition to delivery tickets and/or invoices for each individual purchase. Before the monthly statement is paid, the items on it should be checked against the individual invoices for correctness and to make sure that no item on the statement has already been paid on the basis of its invoice. Any balance brought forward from an earlier month should also be carefully checked to make sure that it is correct and has not already been paid.

Reconciling Your Bank Statement

The bank will periodically send you your canceled checks and a statement of your bank account. Some banks send out statements once a month, on various days of the month. Others, particularly in the case of accounts without much activity, send out statements less often. However, you can arrange with your bank to have your statement sent each month as of the last business day of the month. This will make it easier for you to *reconcile* your records with the bank statement—that is, to compare the two records and account for any differences.

Reconciling your bank statement every month without fail is an important step in keeping accurate records. Even if someone else does the rest of your recordkeeping, you should do the bank reconciliation yourself. How this is done is explained in detail in part 4.

Part 3 | Lining Up the Records

The Sales and Cash Receipts Journal................... 25

    Entries From the Daily Summary....................... 25

    Miscellaneous Receipts.................................. 27

    Entries From Other Sources............................ 27

    Checking Your Entries.................................. 27

    Filing the Records..................................... 28

    Preparing the Monthly Totals........................... 28

Cash Disbursements, Purchases, and Expense Journal... 28

    Payroll Entries.. 29

    Owners' Withdrawals.................................... 29

    Month's End Procedures................................ 33

The Sales and Cash Receipts Journal

The *Daily Summary of Sales and Cash Receipts* is in effect a worksheet for figuring and recording the results of a single day's business. The *Sales and Cash Receipts Journal* brings together on one page the information from a number of *Daily Summaries*. This provides a better permanent record and makes the information easier to work with for various purposes. Some entries on a typical page from a *Sales and Cash Receipts Journal* are shown as exhibit 4.

Entries From the Daily Summary

Usually, total sales, charge sales, collections on account, and the total cash deposit can all be entered on the same line of the journal. The date should be entered, "Daily Summary" written in the description column, and the money amounts entered from the summary to the corresponding journal columns. Note that each column is marked "Dr." or "Cr." to indicate whether the entries in that column are normally debit or credit entries. If it is necessary to make a debit entry in a credit column or a credit entry in a debit column, that entry is circled or written in red. When the columns are totaled, these entries will be subtracted instead of added.

Illustration 1 on exhibit 4 shows the entries that would be made in the *Sales and Cash Receipts Journal* from the *Daily Summary of Sales and Cash Receipts* shown in exhibit 3. The amounts entered under Total Sales, Collections on Account, and Total Cash Deposit are taken from the *Daily Summary* items having the same identification as the journal columns. The amount entered under Charges to Customers is from item 13, Charge Sales, of the *Daily Summary*.

If you have provided separate lines on the *Daily Summary* for receipts from sources other than sales or collections on account, you should have corresponding columns in the *Sales and Cash Receipts Journal*. These columns should follow the Collections-on-Account column, and they will be "Cr." columns.

Exhibit 4.—Sales and Cash Receipts Journal

Date	PR	Description and/or Account	Total Sales (CR)	Charges to Customers (DR)	Collections on Account (CR)	Miscellaneous Income and Expense Items (DR)	Miscellaneous Income and Expense Items (CR)	General Ledger Items (DR)	General Ledger Items (CR)	Total Cash Deposit (DR)
19—										
Illustration I: Entries from exhibit 3										
Mar 23		Daily Summary	660 00	225 00	100 00					544 00
		Refund on merchandise					15 00			
		Cash short				6 00				
Illustration II: Entries from exhibit 16										
Mar 23		Daily Summary	660 00	225 00	100 00					562 00
		Refund on merchandise					15 00			
		Cash short				6 00				
		Exchange							18 00	

As each day's entries are made in the journal, the amount entered in the Total-Cash-Deposit column is also entered as a deposit in your checkbook and added to the previous balance.

Miscellaneous Receipts

Items included in "Miscellaneous receipts" on the *Daily Summary* and itemized on the back of the summary sheet must be identified in the description column of the *Sales and Cash Receipts Journal*. They will therefore need separate lines. The amounts are entered under General Ledger Items or under Miscellaneous Income and Expense Items.

Miscellaneous receipts that represent either refunds on expense items or income not due to sales are entered in the *credit* column under Miscellaneous Income and Expense Items. This includes receipts from such sources as rent collections, interest, refunds from suppliers, advertising rebates, and so on. Cash over and cash short are also entered here— cash over as a *credit* and cash short as a *debit*.

Miscellaneous receipts that do not represent income or expense items are entered in the *credit* column under General Ledger Items. This might include such receipts as additional investment in the business or a loan from your bank. In most small businesses, the General-Ledger column of the *Sales and Cash Receipts Journal* is seldom used.

Entries From Other Sources

Cash receipts are sometimes entered in the journal from sources other than the *Daily Summary*. For example, if your banker grants you a loan, he will probably just credit the amount of the loan to your bank account and send you a notice that this has been done. Since no cash is actually received as part of the day's operations, the money need not be included in your *Daily Summary*. It can be entered directly in the journal. The description will be "Notes payable—bank loan," and the amount will be entered under Total Cash Deposit and in the *credit* column under General Ledger Items.

Another example is a transaction that you do not want to appear in the *Daily Summary* because you wish to keep it confidential—for instance, the investment of additional capital in the business. A separate deposit can be prepared and entered in the journal.

Checking Your Entries

After the day's entries in the *Sales and Cash Receipts Journal* have been made, the work should be checked by adding all entries in the *debit* columns and all entries in the *credit* columns. The two totals should be the same.

Since the *Daily Summary* has already been checked. any errors here are simply mistakes in transferring the figures from the summary to the journal. They can easily be found and corrected.

Filing the Records

When these steps have been completed, charge-sales tickets and records of collections on account are put aside to be recorded in the individual customer accounts as explained in part 7. The *Daily Summary*, cash-register tapes, cash sales tickets, adding-machine tapes, and any other written records used in the balancing are filed by date.

Preparing the Monthly Totals

At the end of the month, each column in the journal is totaled, and the totals are checked in the way described for daily entries. The Miscellaneous-Income-and-Expense entries and the General-Ledger entries are summarized so as to give a single figure for each account or type of expense appearing in the columns. Cash overages and shortages are combined to give the net cash overage or shortage for the month.

It is a good idea to enter the column totals lightly in pencil until you have reconciled your bank statement, as explained in part 4. After you have made any adjustments or corrections made necessary by the reconciliation, the column totals should be entered in ink.

The Cash Disbursements, Purchases, and Expense Journal

Daily, if possible, the checks drawn should be entered in the *Cash Disbursements, Purchases, and Expense Journal* (exhibit 5). Be careful to see that *every check number* is accounted for in the journal. If a check is spoiled, write "VOID" in the payee column, enter the check number, and leave all other columns blank. Some typical entries are shown in illustration I of exhibit 5. (Entries shown in illustrations II and III of exhibit 5 are described in subsequent parts of this booklet.)

The *Cash Disbursements, Purchases, and Expense Journal* shown in exhibit 5 has a minimum number of columns. It is quite possible, for instance, that you will need more than two columns for payroll deductions. Also, if some types of expense normally require several payments a month (for instance, operating supplies, delivery expense, postage) additional columns should be provided for them. Expenses that normally have only one or two payments a month (such as rent, telephone, electricity, and so on) are entered in the *debit* column under Miscellaneous Income and Expense Items with the account shown for each.

The General-Ledger columns of the *Cash Disbursements Journal* are used only for entries that directly affect the assets, liabilities, and capital of the business as recorded in the *General Ledger* (explained in part 6). Some examples are purchases of furniture or equipment, payment of bank loans, drawings of the proprietor or partners, and so on.

Some checks may include disbursements that are chargeable to more than one account—petty-cash checks, for instance. In such a case, the amount chargeable to each account—for example, postage, small purchases of supplies, minor repairs—is recorded on the supporting document and on the check stub and entered in the proper column of the journal. If this results in more than one entry in the same column, a separate line is used for each entry. The next check is then entered on the next *unused* line.

Payroll Entries

You will note that columns are shown for gross salaries and for Federal income tax and Social Security deductions. In some areas, a State or local payroll tax may also have to be withheld. Or you may have other payroll deductions such as for group hospitalization or savings bonds. A column should be provided for each type of deduction.

In some localities and types of businesses, salaries are paid in cash rather than by check. In such cases, one check should be drawn to "Payroll" for the total net pay and cashed at the bank. The cash is then distributed to the employees in pay envelopes showing gross pay, deductions, and net pay. A signed receipt should be required from each employee. The entries in the *Cash Disbursements Journal*, taken from a payroll summary, are the same as when payment is made by check except that only one check number will be shown. Payroll records and payroll taxes are discussed further in part 10.

Owner's Withdrawals

If your business is an individual proprietorship or a partnership and you or other partners withdraw fixed amounts regularly as "salaries,"

(*Please turn to page 32.*)

Exhibit 5.—Cash Disbursements, Purchases, and Expense Journal

Date	Payee and/or Account	Ch. No.	Amount of Check (CR)	Merchandise Purchases (DR)	Gross Salaries (DR)	Payroll Deductions Income Tax (CR)	Payroll Deductions Soc. Sec. (CR)	Miscellaneous Income and Expense Items (DR)	Miscellaneous Income and Expense Items (CR)	General Ledger Items (DR)	General Ledger Items (CR)
19—											
Jul 1	John Smith—Rent	92	200 00					200 00			
14	ABC Company	93	115 00	115 00							
19	Z Company—Furn. & Fix.	94	30 00							30 00	
	VOID	95									
20	Payroll	96	50 85		58 50	5 90	1 75				

Illustration I: Miscellaneous entries—rent, merchandise purchase, asset purchase, spoiled check, payroll

Illustration II: Accounts payable

A—Accounts payable recorded

Jul	31	Accounts payable		275 00		300 00
		Furniture & Fixtures			25 00	25 00

B—Accounts payable reversed

Aug	1	Accounts payable		(275 00)	300 00	
		Furniture & Fixtures				25 00

C—Accounts payable paid

Aug	5	Z Company—Furn. & Fix.	101	25 00	25 00	
	7	ABC Company	102	175 00	175 00	
	12	XY Corporation	103	100 00	100 00	

Illustration III: Check to restore change fund when checks cashed for customers total more than receipts to be deposited

Aug	18	Exchange	111	18 00	18 00

these withdrawals are not treated as employees' salaries. They should *not* be entered in the Gross-Salaries column. They are not subject as salaries to Federal withholding or Social Security taxes, although they could be subject to other payroll deductions. They are described as "Proprietor's Drawings" and entered either in the General-Ledger *debit* column or in a separate column if their frequency justifies it. If there are partners, a separate drawing account is maintained for each.

When payroll deductions are made from the proprietor's drawings, enter (1) the amount of the check, (2) the deductions, and (3) proprietor's drawings equal to the amount of the check *plus* the deductions.

If your business is a corporation, you are an employee, and any salary paid you is treated just like that paid other employees.

Merchandise withdrawn by the owner. If your business handles consumer goods, you and your family are probably among its "customers." You may be tempted to take the items you need out of stock without making any record of them. But you should not do this, any more than you should take cash from your cash register without a record.

There are several reasons for this. For one thing, withdrawing merchandise without recording it has the effect of reducing the profits of your business—and hence your income taxes. In effect, it gives you a tax deduction for personal living expenses. Naturally, the Internal Revenue Service takes a dim view of such a procedure. It is one of the matters IRS men particularly look into when they examine the income-tax returns of a small business. Not recording merchandise taken from stock also distorts the operating results of the business and increases inventory shortages.

On the other hand, withdrawals of merchandise for your personal use should not be treated as ordinary sales. To do this would result in including "profits" on these withdrawals in income of the business and would increase your income tax unnecessarily. To prevent this, merchandise withdrawn for your own use should be recorded at cost rather than at selling price. Also, it is best to treat it as a deduction from purchases rather than as a sale at cost value, since the latter would tend to distort your gross margin.

If the withdrawals are only occasional, they can be entered individually in the *Cash Disbursements, Purchases, and Expense Journal* by a *deduction* (circled or in red) in the Merchandise-Purchases column and a *debit* entry in the General-Ledger column, with the account designated as "Drawing Account," or "Proprietor's Drawings." If withdrawals are frequent, a tally can be kept throughout the month and only one entry made in the journal at the end of the month.

For a discussion of how to arrive at the cost, see "Merchandise Inventories," in part 4. If a tally is kept of all withdrawals during the month, it may be easier to keep this by selling price and reduce the total to cost at the end of the month by the gross-margin method explained in part 4.

Month's End Procedures

At the end of the month, each column of the *Cash Disbursements, Purchases, and Expense Journal* is totaled. Items appearing in the Miscellaneous-Income-and-Expense and General-Ledger columns should be summarized so that only one total is shown for each account.

You can check your column totals by adding all debit-column totals and all credit-column totals. The two totals should be the same.

Column totals should be entered lightly in pencil until their accuracy has been further proved by your bank-account reconciliation. After any necessary adjustments or corrections have been made, the final totals should be entered in ink.

Three further steps are needed before you are ready to prepare the monthly financial statements—reconciling your bank account, setting up your accounts payable, and counting or estimating your merchandise inventory. These steps will be discussed next.

Part 4 | Getting Set for Monthly Financial Statements

Reconciling Your Bank Statement...................... 37

    Reconciling Your Record With the Bank's................. 37

    Recording Adjustments.................................. 39

    The Final Check....................................... 40

Recording Accounts Payable.......................... 40

    Setting Up Accounts Payable............................ 41

    Recording Accounts Payable in the Cash Disbursements

    Journal... 41

    Reversing the Entries.................................. 41

    Recording Payment of the Accounts..................... 42

Merchandise Inventories............................. 42

    Estimating the Inventory............................... 42

    Counting the Merchandise.............................. 43

    Pricing the Inventory................................. 45

    Perpetual Inventory Records........................... 46

Reconciling
Your Bank Statement

Before starting to check, or *reconcile,* your bank statement, you should check your own figures. Your *General Ledger* (explained in part 6) will include an account "Cash in Bank." Beginning with the bank balance shown in this account at the end of the preceding month, *add* the total cash deposited during the month and *subtract* the total cash disbursements. (These figures are the penciled totals from the Total-Cash-Deposit column of the *Sales and Cash Receipts Journal* and the Amount-of-Check column of the *Cash Disbursements, Purchases, and Expense Journal.*)

The result should agree with your checkbook balance at the end of the month. If it does not, an error has been made in entering or adding one or more items in either the checkbook or the journals. Such errors can be found by taking the following steps:

1. Add check amounts recorded on check stubs to make sure that the total agrees with the Amount-of-Check column of the *Cash Disbursements Journal.* If it does not, check the individual amounts.

2. Add the deposit amounts recorded on the check stubs to make sure that the total agrees with the Total-Cash-Deposit column of the *Cash Receipts Journal.* If it does not, check the individual amounts.

3. Recompute the running balance in your checkbook to make sure that the additions and subtractions are correct.

Reconciling Your Record With the Bank's

When you are sure that the balance in your checkbook is mathematically correct, you are ready to reconcile your record with the bank's. You will need the preceding month's reconciliation, the checkbook stubs, and the canceled checks and bank statement received from the bank. Then take these steps:

1. Arrange all the canceled checks in numerical order.

2. Compare deposits listed on the bank statement with deposits entered in your checkbook. List in the first section of the reconciliation

(exhibit 6) any deposits recorded in your checkbook during the month but not appearing on the bank statement. (If deposits are made daily, only one or two deposits at the end of the month should have to be put on this list.)

3. There will probably be some canceled checks from the previous month. Check these off on the list of outstanding checks shown on the preceding month's reconciliation. List in the first section of the current reconciliation the checks still outstanding.

4. Check off on the corresponding check stubs all canceled checks drawn during the month being reconciled. Add the checks recorded on the remaining stubs to the list of outstanding checks on the reconciliation. (Disregard any checks that you may have written after the end of the month.)

Exhibit 6

Bank Reconciliation November 30, 19—

Balance per bank statement.....................		$793.74
Add deposits not credited:		
November 29........................	$247.52	
November 30........................	302.19	549.71
		$1,343.45
Deduct outstanding checks:		
No. 913—10/20.....................	$30.18	
929—11/15.....................	10.14	
935—11/25.....................	142.60	
939—11/30.....................	82.60	
940—11/30.....................	95.80	
941—11/30.....................	74.50	435.82
Adjusted balance per bank statement.............		$907.63
Balance per checkbook.........................		$903.38
Add:		
Check No. 920 entered as $58.30 should be $53.80........................	$4.50	
Deposits of Nov. 1 recorded as $298.60 should be $299.60................	1.00	5.50
		$908.88
Deduct bank service charge.....................		1.25
Adjusted balance per checkbook.................		$907.63

5. If any errors in amounts are discovered in the preceding steps, list them in the second section of the reconciliation statement as adjustments to be added or deducted.

6. Examine the bank statement for service charges or other adjustments to your account and enter them in the second section of the reconciliation.

7. Carry out the additions and subtractions shown on the bank reconciliation. The adjusted balance per bank statement should equal the adjusted balance per your checkbook.

Errors made by the bank. Occasionally, you may find that the bank has made a mistake in your account. The following types of errors can occur:

Deposit or check of another person posted to your account.
Your deposit or check posted to another person's account.
Deposit or check posted in the wrong amount.
Preceding month's balance incorrectly brought forward on your
  bank statement.
Addition or subtraction incorrectly carried out on the bank
  statement.

Any such errors should be reported to the bank at once. They must also be shown as adjustment items in the first section of your bank reconciliation. When the next month's bank statement is received, make sure that any bank errors from the previous month have been corrected in the statement.

Recording Adjustments

Any adjustments to your own records made in reconciling your bank statement must be entered in your checkbook and also in the journals, as follows:

If a check was recorded in the wrong amount:

Enter the amount of the adjustment in the Amount-of-Check column of the *Cash Disbursements Journal* with an explanation.

Enter the same amount in the other column in which the check was originally entered.

If the check was recorded as *less* than the correct amount, simply enter the adjustment in the two columns. This will have the effect of an *addition*. If the check was recorded as *more* than the correct amount, enter the adjustment as a *deduction* (circled or in red).

If the second entry is in the Miscellaneous-Income-and-Expense column or the General-Ledger Column, the adjustment will be entered there as a *debit* if the check was recorded as *less* than the correct amount; as a *credit* if it was recorded as *more* than the correct amount.

If a deposit was recorded in the wrong amount:
Enter the amount of the adjustment in the Total-Cash-Deposit column of the *Cash Receipts Journal.*

If the adjustment can be identified with a specific receipt, it should also be entered in the column for that type of receipt. It is more likely, however, that the error was made in balancing the day's work. In that case, it should be entered as a shortage or overage.

If *too small* an amount was recorded for the deposit, the adjustment should be entered in the journal as an *addition;* if *too large* an amount, as a *deduction.* If the second entry is in the Miscellaneous-Income-and-Expense or General-Ledger column, the adjustment will be entered there as a *credit* if the amount recorded for the deposit was *too small;* as a *debit* if the amount recorded was *too large.*

Bank *service charges* are entered in the Amount-of-Check column of the *Cash Disbursements Journal* and as a debit in the Miscellaneous-Income-and-Expense-Items column. Your checkbook balance should be corrected by adding or subtracting the net adjustment.

The Final Check

When all adjustments have been recorded and the corrected totals of the two journals "inked in" and posted to the *General Ledger*, the balance of the Cash-in-Bank account of the ledger should agree with the adjusted balance shown on the bank reconciliation.

Recording Accounts Payable

Since inventories are an important factor in accounting for the income of a store, Internal Revenue regulations require that you record merchandise purchases on an accrual basis. This means that you must *set up accounts payable* for all purchases that have not been paid for. For income-tax purposes, you only need to record accounts payable at the end of the year. For your own purposes, it is best to set them up at the end of each month in order to keep your monthly statements from being distorted.

Setting Up Accounts Payable

You should have an unpaid-bills file into which all delivery tickets or invoices for charge purchases are put.   If you do not receive an invoice or delivery ticket, make a memo of the purchase and put it in the file. All unpaid statements from vendors should also be kept in this file.

When a bill is paid, all delivery tickets, invoices, and statements having to do with it are taken from the file and kept as supporting documents of the payment.   Thus, at any time, the items in the unpaid file represent all purchases that have not been paid for.

At the end of the month, a list of the unpaid items is drawn up, showing vendors and amounts.   The amounts are then added to give the total accounts payable for that month.   If any items are represented only by delivery tickets or memos with no price given, an estimate of the price should be made and used in listing the accounts payable.

If most of the vendors will be the same each month, you can make the accounts-payable listing on multicolumn paper and use a column for each month.   This has two advantages over a separate listing for each month.   It saves rewriting most of the vendors' names, and it gives you a month-to-month comparison of your accounts payable.

Recording Accounts Payable in the Cash Disbursements Journal

The total of the accounts payable is entered in the *Cash Disbursements, Purchases, and Expense Journal.*   If only merchandise purchases are involved, enter the total in the Merchandise-Purchases column and in the General-Ledger credit column, with the account shown as "Accounts Payable."   If other items are involved, they will be entered in the columns to which they apply (usually as a debit in the General-Ledger or Miscellaneous-Income-and-Expense-Items column) with the account shown.   In either case, the total of the accounts payable is entered as a credit in the General-Ledger column.   (See entry A dated July 31, in illustration II of exhibit 5.)

The effect of these entries is to include all purchases in the month in which they were made, whether or not they have been paid for.   The entries may be made either before or after the bank reconciliation, since cash is not affected.

Reversing the Entries

If nothing further were done about them, the entries described above would require special handling of checks written during the next month to pay any of the accounts included in the total.   This can be avoided by *reversing* the accounts-payable entries.   Under this method, the first entry in the *Cash Disbursements, Purchases, and Expense Journal* each month is the reverse, or opposite, of the accounts-payable entry made in the preceding month. This means that the amounts entered in the preceding month as additions will now be entered in the same columns as deductions; those entered as debits will now be entered as credits. The accounts-payable total entered in the General-Ledger column as a credit is now entered in that column as a debit. (Note how the August 1 entry B in exhibit 5 "reverses" the July 31 entry.)

Recording Payments of the Accounts

When checks are drawn to pay for purchases included in the preceding month's accounts payable, they are entered like any other check. Each of these purchases will thus have been *added twice* (once as an account payable and once as a disbursement) and *deducted once* (as a reversing entry). This has the effect of leaving the purchase as a charge in the month in which the purchase was made even though the check is drawn and recorded in the following month. Study the entries in illustration II of exhibit 5.

Merchandise Inventories

One of the most important steps in the preparation of financial statements is the obtaining of accurate inventory figures. There are a number of methods of keeping *perpetual* or *book inventories,* but a really accurate inventory can be obtained only by counting all the merchandise on hand—*a physical inventory.* If a book inventory has been kept also, a comparison of the two inventories may reveal inventory shortages or overages.

Many small merchants, however, do not want to take on the clerical work of maintaining perpetual inventory records. At the same time, they do not feel that a physical inventory every month is justified. In such cases, the inventory can be estimated for monthly statements and a physical inventory taken only at the end of the year.

Estimating the Inventory

Inventory can be estimated by the gross-margin method. Under this method, you assume that the gross margin (sales less cost of goods sold) for the period is going to be a certain percentage of your sales. The gross-margin percent for the period between the last two physical inventories is most often used for this. The cost of sales for the current period will then be the cost-of-sales percent (100 percent less the gross-margin percent) times the sales for the period. Ending inventory is then computed as in the following example.

Suppose that your sales for the month are $10,000, that your inventory at the beginning of the month was $3,000, and that your merchandise purchases during the month amount to $6,000. You estimate your gross margin at 25 percent of sales. Your ending inventory can be computed as follows:

Beginning inventory	$3,000	
Merchandise purchases	6,000	
Merchandise available for sale		$9,000
Estimated gross-margin percent	25	
Cost-of-sales percent (100–25)	75	
Sales for the month	$10,000	
Cost of goods sold (75 percent of $10,000)		7,500
Ending inventory		$1,500

If you use the gross-margin method of computing your inventory, it should be applied separately to each department. This method can give fairly accurate results for monthly financial statements under some circumstances, but the fact remains that it produces only an estimated inventory. As often as practicable, you should make a physical count rather than an estimate.

An alternative to a complete physical inventory every month is to count some departments each month and use the gross-margin method for other departments. The departments are scheduled so that each one is counted every 2 or 3 months.

Counting the Merchandise

How often should you take a *physical inventory*—actually count the items on your shelves? That depends on the type of business you are in and whether you also have a reliable book-inventory system. In all cases, a physical inventory should be taken at least once a year, usually as of the close of your fiscal year. If accurate book inventories cannot be maintained, a monthly physical inventory may be needed for financial statements. In some businesses or departments where turnover is rapid, a weekly physical inventory is helpful, although usually such an inventory would not be converted to dollars

Preparations for taking inventory. To ensure accuracy in counting, care should be taken to see that merchandise is in good order in the shelves, bins, or compartments. It is often impractical to try to take an accurate inventory during business hours, so the actual counting must usually be done in the evening or over a weekend. However, the orderly arranging of merchandise, instructions to the counters, and perhaps the counting of reserve stock should be done ahead of time.

A part of your planning for taking inventory should be to establish shipping and receiving "cutoffs"—that is, to make certain (1) that all items entered in your books as purchased before the inventory have been received and are counted, if still on hand; and (2) that all items recorded as sold before the inventory are removed and not counted.

If the type of merchandise you are counting requires weighing or any other kind of measuring, the equipment that will be needed for this should be on hand.

The tally sheets. In some types of business, a complete description of each item by brand, container size, and so on is needed. In these cases, inventory tally sheets showing this information should be prepared in advance, so that the only writing necessary is to record the quantities counted. These sheets should have space for inserting the unit prices and extending the dollar value of the stock. The order of the items on the list should follow as closely as possible the order in which the stock is arranged in the store. Separate sheets should be prepared for separate departments.

If you think you do not need tally sheets, you can take inventory on "tags." A tag is placed with each different item in stock before the count. The description of the item and the number of units in stock are then entered on the tag by the counters. Here, too, it is advisable to have a space on the tag for the price and extension.

If a great many tags or tallies are used, they should be numbered. This is necessary to make sure that none are lost or misplaced after the count is made and before the final summarizing of the inventory valuation. Tag or tally numbers can also be used to identify the department involved.

In some cases, a complete description of the items is not necessary; the number of items and the price might be enough for the counters to enter. The department should always be identified, however, by marking or physical separation of the tags or tallies.

Counting by teams. It may be helpful to have one person count and call to another person who does the writing. Sometimes, to ensure accuracy, a second person or team counts the items again. If this is done, the tag or tally may be left with the merchandise after the first count, to be removed after the final count. Or a duplicate sheet or tag stub can be used for the second count, to get a completely independent check. The two counts should then be compared, and any discrepancies corrected by a third count.

If you have a number of people taking part in your inventory, you may want to have the names or initials of persons counting, listing, and/or checking entered on each tag or tally.

Pricing the Inventory

After the physical counting of your inventory has been finished, each item must be priced. A generally accepted method of pricing inventories is valuation of the items at cost or market, whichever is lower.

Cost is the price for which you purchased the item. Theoretically, this would be the invoice price, plus freight-in, less any discounts taken. In a small retail business, however, the factor of freight-in would generally not be material and could probably be ignored. Discounts would probably not be significant, either. If a small cash discount is applicable to most of your purchases, you could make a percentage reduction in the overall inventory rather than try to reduce the price of the individual items.

Market value would be one of the following:

1. The replacement price of the item.
2. If the item has been marked down, your current asking price, less your normal gross margin.
3. Scrap or salvage value if the item is no longer salable at retail.

The retail method of valuing inventory. You can avoid computing the cost of each item by using the *retail method* of valuing your inventory. Under this method, retail prices of the items are entered on the tally sheet or tag as the count is made. The retail value of the inventory for each department is then totaled and reduced by the year-to-date gross-margin percent for the department.

In the case of marked-down items, the marked-down retail price should be used. (All appropriate markdowns should be made before taking the inventory.) If any unsalable merchandise is on hand, it should not be included in this computation, but should be valued at scrap or salvage value, if any.

Some types of merchandise, such as meats and fresh produce, fluctuate so widely in price that the retail method of pricing cannot be used. Fortunately, there are usually not too many different items on hand in these departments. Pricing them at your current cost is not difficult.

Coded costs. Another method of determining cost prices for inventory valuation is to have the merchandise marked with a coded cost as well as a retail price at the time it is put on sale. A letter code can be devised by using a 10-letter key word with no letter repeated, for example:

1 2 3 4 5 6 7 8 9 0

P U R C H A S I N G

Thus an article that cost $3.17 and sells for $5.00 would be marked "RPS $5.00." In taking inventory, the counters enter the decoded cost price on the tag or tally.

The practice of marking merchandise with a coded cost is common in gift shops, jewelry stores, and other stores where turnover is comparatively slow and items have a rather high gross margin and unit value. It serves primarily as a guide to management in making markdowns and sometimes in bargaining with customers. Its use in inventory valuation is limited by (1) the work involved in coding the merchandise in the first place, and (2) the fact that decoding of prices by the inventory takers can be troublesome and subject to errors. Also, the work must be reviewed to make certain that no cost prices are higher than market.

Total dollar valuation. After all inventory items have been priced, the total dollar values are found by multiplying the prices by the quantities. This is usually done on the tag or tally sheets containing the quantities counted. The amounts on the tags or tally sheets for each department are then added to give the total for the department. *Accuracy is important.* It is advisable to have the work checked for clerical and arithmetical errors.

Perpetual Inventory Records

Some merchants keep a continuous, or perpetual, book record of their inventory. This method is described here only briefly. If you want to use it, you should have a qualified accountant set up the system for you and explain its use in detail.

One type of perpetual inventory involves keeping records at both retail selling price and cost. To the beginning inventory at retail prices, purchases are added (with each invoice priced at the expected selling price) and all sales and markdowns are deducted. This results in a perpetual inventory "at retail." At any time, this inventory can be converted to cost as follows: Divide total purchases at cost by total purchases at retail, and multiply the inventory balance by the result.

If these records are carefully kept, they provide a very accurate theoretical inventory. Inventory shortages will not be disclosed, however. A physical count is still necessary at least once a year.

Part 5	The Score— Win or Lose, and How Much?

The Profit-and-Loss Statement........................ 49

    Where the Figures Come From......................... 52

    Posting References....................................... 53

    The Year to Date....................................... 53

    The Percentages.. 54

Departmental Operating Records...................... 54

    Departmental Purchases and Sales Record................. 55

    Statement of Departmental Operations.................... 56

The Profit-and-Loss Statement

As soon as possible after the end of the month, you should have completed the following procedures, or as many of them as apply to your business. (Page numbers refer to the pages in this book on which the procedures are explained.)

1. Entered all cash transactions in the *Sales and Cash Receipts Journal* (p. 25) and the *Cash Disbursements, Purchases, and Expense Journal* (p. 28).

2. Reconciled your bank account (p. 37).

3. Established the amount of your accounts payable and entered it in the *Cash Disbursements, Purchases, and Expense Journal* (p. 40).

4. Billed your customers (p. 77) and balanced your accounts receivable (p. 77).

5. Established the amount of your ending inventory (p. 42).

6. Made any necessary noncash entries, such as allowance for bad debts (p. 83) and depreciation (p. 106).

7. Totaled and balanced your journals (pp. 28 and 33).

If you keep your records by departments, you should also have posted your Departmental Purchases and Sales Record and prepared your Statement of Departmental Operations. (These records will be discussed in the next section, beginning on p. 54).

You are now ready to prepare your monthly financial statements—the *Profit-and-Loss Statement* and the *Balance Sheet*—and to post your *General Ledger*. (The Balance Sheet and the *General Ledger* are discussed in part 6.)

Exhibit 7 shows a typical Profit-and-Loss Statement for a single proprietorship or partnership. This statement shows the results of operations for the month and for the year to date, with percentages based on net sales. The list of expenses is only a suggestion. You can add or delete items according to the requirements of your business.

(*Please turn to page 52.*)

Exhibit 7

Statement of Profit and Loss

XYZ STORE

Month of _____ 19__ and ____ months ended _____, 19__

	This month		Year to date	
	Amount	Percent of sales	Amount	Percent of sales
1. Net sales...............	$	100	$	100
Less cost of goods sold:				
2. Beginning inventory.... 1ˢᵗ day	$		$	
3. Merchandise purchases......				
4. Merchandise available for sale..	$		$	
5. Less ending inventory. end of year				
6. Cost of goods sold......	$		$	
7. Gross margin...........	$		$	
Less expenses:				
8. Salaries and wages......				
9. Rent................	$		$	

10.	Utilities	
11.	Repairs and maintenance	
12.	Delivery expense	
13.	Supplies	
14.	Advertising	
15.	Depreciation	
16.	Bad debts	
17.	Taxes and licenses	
18.	Insurance	
19.	Interest	
20.	Other expense	$
21.	Total expenses	$
22.	Operating profit (loss)	$
23.	Other income	
24.	Net profit (loss)	$

Where the Figures Come From

Amounts in the This-Month column of exhibit 7 are determined as follows:

LINE 1, *Net sales.* Enter the total of the column headed "Total Sales" in the *Sales and Cash Receipts Journal* less any debits to Sales from the summary of the Miscellaneous-Income-and-Expense-Items column in the *Cash Disbursements Journal.*

LINE 2, *Beginning inventory.* Enter the ending inventory of the previous month from the inventory account in the *General Ledger.*

LINE 3, *Purchases.* Enter the month's total from the Merchandise-Purchases column of the *Cash Disbursements Journal* less any *credits* to purchases from the summary of the Miscellaneous-Income-and-Expense-Items column in the *Cash Receipts Journal.*

LINE 4, *Merchandise available for sale.* Add purchases to beginning inventory (line 2 plus line 3).

LINE 5, *Ending inventory.* Enter the total ending inventory found by using one of the methods explained in part 4.

LINE 6, *Cost of goods sold.* Enter merchandise available for sale less ending inventory (line 4 less line 5).

LINE 7, *Gross margin.* Enter net sales less cost of goods sold (line 1 less line 6).

LINE 8, *Salaries and wages.* Enter total of the Gross-Salaries column in the *Cash Disbursements Journal.*

LINES 9 THROUGH 20, *Expenses.* Enter amounts from the summary of the Miscellaneous-Income-and-Expense-Items column in the *Cash Disbursements Journal* (debits) less any credits to the same expenses from the corresponding column in the *Cash Receipts Journal.* (You may have provided separate columns in the *Cash Disbursements Journal* for some recurring expenses. If so, enter the totals of these columns, less any credits, on the proper lines.)

LINE 21, *Total expenses.* Enter the total of the expenses recorded on lines 8 through 20.

LINE 22, *Operating profit (or loss).* Gross margin less total expenses (line 7 less line 21; if the business suffers a loss, line 21 less line 7).

LINE 23, *Other income.* Enter any income items not already taken care of from the summary of the Miscellaneous-Income-and-Expense-Items column in the *Cash Receipts Journal* less any debits to the same categories from the corresponding column in the *Cash Disbursements Journal.*

You may have provided separate columns in the *Sales and Cash Receipts Journal* for recurring items of other income. If you want your Profit-and-Loss Statement also to show some types of "other income" separately, more than one line can be used.

LINE 24, *Net profit.* Operating profit plus other income (line 22 plus line 23).

If your business is a corporation, line 24 will read, "Net profit before income taxes," and two lines will be added:

LINE 25, *Income taxes.* Enter from the Miscellaneous-Income-and-Expense-Items column of the *Cash Disbursements Journal.*

LINE 26, *Net profit.* Net profit before income taxes less income taxes (line 24 less line 25).

Posting References

As each amount is entered from its journal to a line on the Profit-and-Loss Statement, a checkmark ($\sqrt{}$) should be made beside the amount in the journal. After all lines on the Profit-and-Loss Statement have been entered, the journals should be reviewed to make sure that the totals of the following columns have checkmarks:

The Total-Sales column in the *Cash Receipts Journal.*

The Merchandise-Purchases and Gross-Salaries columns in the *Cash Disbursements Journal.*

The summaries of the Miscellaneous-Income-and-Expense-Items columns in both journals.

Any additional columns you have provided for other income or expense items.

The Year to Date

Before going on with the Profit-and-Loss Statement, you should post your *General Ledger* as described in part 6. The balancing of the ledger will prove the accuracy of all your entries up to this point, and you will then be ready to go on to the year-to-date and percentage columns on your Profit-and-loss Statement.

For the first month of the year, the figures for the year to date will be identical to those for the month. For all other months, each year-to-date figure will equal the current month's figure plus the year-to-date figure from the preceding month's statement.

Exceptions to this are figures having to do with beginning and ending inventories. Beginning inventory in the year-to-date column remains the same throughout the year. It is always the beginning inventory established at the beginning of the year. Merchandise available for sale in the year-to-date column is always beginning inventory plus the year-to-date merchandise purchases. Ending inventory in the year-to-date column is the same as that in the month's column.

54

The Percentages

The percentages are obtained by dividing each amount by the net sales for the period. Percentages are not usually computed for lines 2 through 5; and if you do not have a calculator, they can also be omitted for the individual expenses. Percentages can then be computed only for lines 6, 21, and 23 (and for corporations, line 25). The percentages for the remaining items can be found by adding or subtracting. When this is done, each net-profit percentage should be checked by dividing the net-profit dollar figure by the corresponding net sales figure.

It should be noted that percentages in the year-to-date column *must be computed*. They cannot be found by adding the month's percentages to the year-to-date percentages from the preceding month, as was done with the dollar amounts.

Departmental Operating Records

If you sell several different types of merchandise, you will find it helpful to organize your operations and your recordkeeping by departments. The primary purpose of this is to get a better picture of your operating results. Even though your overall operations may be profitable, you may find, by keeping departmental records, that one department is producing most of the profits while others are barely breaking even or perhaps even losing money. You can then attack the problem of what to do to improve the profit of the departments with a poor showing. You may even decide to drop a department or reduce its activities.

There are other advantages to keeping records by departments. Many statistics about typical operations are available through trade associations, governmental publications, and so on. These statistics can be very useful in finding weak spots in your own store's performance. But they are published on a departmental basis. Unless your business is largely a one-department operation, they would be useless for comparison with figures covering your whole store.

Gross-margin percentages from departmental records can be used to estimate inventories by the gross-margin method (part 4) where an overall percentage could be misleading. Also, items subject to a sales or excise tax can be segregated from items not subject to such taxes.

How far you want to departmentalize will depend on the size and nature of your business. A grocery store, for example, might have some or all of the following departments: fresh produce, meats, bakery products, dairy products, frozen foods, dry groceries, and taxable items (if you are in a jurisdiction where foods are not taxed). A drugstore, with the many products carried today, might have any number of departments. Don't overdo it, though. A specific type of merchandise or service should not be set up as a separate department unless the volume of sales justifies such a separation.

Departmental Purchases and Sales Record

The basic tool for breaking down your records by departments is a *Departmental Purchases and Sales Record* (exhibit 8). The departments are identified here by numbers to give the illustration more general application, but you will probably find it more satisfactory to name the departments. Also, if you have many departments, one page may be used for purchases and another page for sales.

Entering departmental purchases. The amount entered in the total purchases column of the Departmental Purchases and Sales Record should, of course, equal the sum of the amounts entered for the individual departments. It should also agree with the merchandise purchases for that day shown in the *Cash Disbursements Journal.*

The breakdown by departments is obtained by analyzing the invoices paid or set up as accounts payable. Each invoice should be marked to show to which department it is charged. In some cases, one invoice

Exhibit 8.—Departmental Purchases and Sales Record

		Purchases			Sales		
Date	Explanation	Total	Dept. 1	Dept. 2	Total	Dept. 1	Dept. 2

may be distributed to more than department. In that case, the amount charged to each department should be shown on the invoice.

Entering departmental sales. The breakdown of sales by departments is obtained from the *Daily Summary of Sales and Cash Receipts,* if shown there, or by analysis of sales checks and/or cash-register tapes. The amount entered in the total-sales column should equal the sum of the entries for the individual departments and should agree with the total sales for that day shown in the *Sales and Cash Receipts Journal.*

Other entries. Occasionally, an entry in the Departmental Purchases and Sales Record may be necessary to record transactions other than purchases or sales. For example, a refund from a vendor might be received and recorded in the *Sales and Cash Receipts Journal* as a reduction in purchases. Or a check might be drawn to a customer as a refund and recorded in the *Cash Disbursements Journal* as a reduction in sales. Since these entries are not routine, they should be entered on a separate line in the Departmental Purchases and Sales Record with explanation.

Monthly totals. At the end of the month, the columns should be added and the totals checked horizontally. That is, the total of the month's purchases for the individual departments should equal the sum of the entries in the total-purchases column, and the total of the month's sales for individual departments should equal the sum of the total-sales column. Also, the total purchases should agree with the month's total of the Merchandise-Purchases column in the *Cash Disbursements, Purchases, and Expense Journal* less any items entered as refunds from suppliers in the *Sales and Cash Receipts Journal.* The total sales should agree with the month's total of the sales column in the *Sales and Cash Receipts Journal* less any items entered as return sales or refunds in the *Cash Disbursements Journal.*

Statement of Departmental Operations

A *Statement of Department Operations* should be prepared at the end of each month. This statement shows totals for the month and for the year to date (see exhibit 9). The sales and purchases for the month are entered directly from the Departmental Purchases and Sales Record. The sales and purchases for the year to date are computed by adding this month's figures to the year-to-date amounts from the previous month's statement.

The beginning inventory for the month is the same as the ending inventory on the previous month's statement. The beginning inventory for the year to date is the inventory as of the beginning of the year and will be the same throughout the year. The ending inventory will be the same for the month and for the year to date. It can be found by one of the methods described in part 4.

The gross-margin amount as computed for the year to date (sales less cost of goods sold) should equal the month's gross margin plus the year-to-date gross margin from the previous month's statement. The gross-margin percent for the month will usually not be exactly the same as the gross-margin percent for the year to date, but if the two percents differ very much, all figures and computations should be checked for accuracy. It is possible, however, that such variations might be due to seasonal clearances, markdowns, and so on.

Direct departmental expenses. The Statement of Departmental Operations may end with the gross-margin percentages. However, if you have expenses that can be assigned to specific departments, you can, if you wish, continue the statement and reduce the gross margin by these direct departmental expenses. This will show the contribution each department makes to overhead expenses and profits.

If this is done, care should be taken to assign expenses fairly. Where a direct expense can easily be assigned to one department, that department should not be penalized just because a corresponding expense cannot be assigned so easily to another department. For example, a butcher's entire salary could probably be assigned to the meat department of a grocery store, while one or more sales clerks serve all the other departments. It would not be right to charge the meat department with the butcher's salary unless the sales clerks' salaries are allocated to the other departments.

The departmental contribution may be more useful than the gross margin of the department. However, you should not complicate your recordkeeping by trying to allocate overhead expenses that are difficult if not impossible to assign accurately.

Using the percentages. Exhibit 9 shows percentages as well as dollars for both gross margins and departmental contributions. The percentages are valuable for comparing your departmental figures with those of other stores, or with your own figures for other periods. In comparing the departments of your store with one another, however, percentages can be misleading, because the gross-margin percent on some types of items is typically lower than on others.

Often a more rapid turnover and other factors make up for a low gross-margin percent. For example, in a small grocery store, the gross margin might be about 16 percent of sales; in a small retail jewelry store, nearly 50 percent of sales. But in the grocery store, inventory would typically "turn over" about once a month; in the jewelry store, only about once a year. Expenses in the grocery store would typically

(*Please turn to page 60.*)

Exhibit 9

Statement of Departmental Operations

YOUR STORE

Month of _____ 19__ and ____ months ended _____, 19__

Item	Total		Department 1		Department 2	
	This month	Year to date	This month	Year to date	This month	Year to date
Net sales...	$____	$____	$____	$____	$____	$____
Less cost of goods sold:						
Inventory at beginning of period...............	$____	$____	$____	$____	$____	$____
Merchandise purchases...........................	____	____	____	____	____	____
Merchandise available for sale..................	$____	$____	$____	$____	$____	$____
(Beginning inventory plus merchandise purchases)						
Less inventory at end of period.................	____	____	____	____	____	____
Cost of goods sold................................	$____	$____	$____	$____	$____	$____
(Merchandise available for sale less less ending inventory)						
Gross margin......................................	$____	$____	$____	$____	$____	$____
(Sales less cost of goods sold)						
Gross margin percent.............................	____	____	____	____	____	____
(Gross margin divided by sales)						

59

(The following is optional)

Direct departmental expenses:					
Salaries and wages	$	$	$	$	$
Rent					
Depreciation of special equipment					
Other					
Total direct departmental expenses	$	$	$	$	$
Departmental contributions	$	$	$	$	$
(Gross margin less direct departmental expenses)					
Departmental contribution percent					
(Departmental contribution divided by sales)					
Turnover per month					

(Cost of goods sold divided by average inventory. In year-to-date column, divide this result by the number of months included. Average inventory is beginning-inventory-plus-ending-inventory divided by 2)

be about 11 percent of sales, leaving a 5 percent net profit; in the jewelry store, expenses would typically be about 46 percent of sales, leaving a net profit of 4 percent. Thus, if you had both a jewelry and a grocery department in your store, it would be unrealistic to compare the gross-margin percents of the two departments.

Departmental turnover. The departmental turnover, which shows how fast your merchandise is moving, is another useful measure for comparing the performance of a department with similar departments in other stores, or the performance of one period with another. It should be noted that the turnover figures in exhibit 9 show monthly turnover. Most published turnover figures are annual. To convert the monthly figures to annual figures, multiply them by 12.

Part 6 | The Shape You're In

The General Ledger and the Balance Sheet............ 63

    Posting From the Sales and Cash Receipts Journal........... 63

    Posting From the Cash Disbursements Journal.............. 63

    Finishing Touches in the Journals and Ledger.............. 64

    Other Postings... 65

    Recording Ending Inventory............................. 65

    Balancing the Ledger.................................... 67

    Preparing the Monthly Balance Sheet..................... 69

Steps To Be Taken at the End of the Year............. 69

    Clearing Away the Deadwood.......................... 70

    Closing the Profit-and-Loss and Proprietor's-Drawings Accounts. 70

    The Final Balance...................................... 71

The General Ledger
and the Balance Sheet

After the income and expense accounts from your journals have been posted to the Profit-and-Loss Statement, you will find that a number of totals in the journals are still unchecked. Most of these will be posted to asset and liability accounts in the *General Ledger*.

An example of a standard *General Ledger* sheet is shown as exhibit 10. A sheet should be provided for each asset, liability, and capital account. Often, each account is given a number for convenience, but this is optional. Exhibit 11 shows a typical chart of accounts for the *General Ledger* of a small store. You may not need all the accounts shown— land and buildings, for instance, if you rent your place of business. On the other hand, you may want to add some accounts.

Posting From the Sales and Cash Receipts Journal

The Total-Sales column and the summary of the Miscellaneous-Income-and-Expense-Items column in the *Cash Receipts Journal* have already been posted to the Profit-and-Loss Statement. The remaining column totals are posted to the *General Ledger* as follows:

The Charges-to-Customers column is posted in the debit column of the Accounts-Receivable account.

The Collections-on-Account total is posted in the credit column of the Accounts-Receivable account.

The General-Ledger columns have already been summarized by accounts. Each net total, debit or credit, is posted in the proper column of the corresponding account in the *General Ledger*.

The Total-Cash-Deposit column is posted in the debit column of the Cash-in-Bank account.

Posting From the Cash Disbursements Journal

The columns headed "Merchandise Purchases," "Gross Salaries," and "Miscellaneous Income and Expense Items" in the *Cash Disbursements*

64

Journal have already been posted to the Profit-and-Loss Statement. The other column totals are posted to the *General Ledger* as follows:

The Amount-of-Check column is entered in the credit column of the Cash-in-Bank account.

Payroll Deductions are entered in the credit columns of the corresponding accounts.

The General Ledger Items, as in the *Cash Receipts Journal*, have already been summarized by accounts. Each net total, debit or credit, is posted to the corresponding *General Ledger* account.

Finishing Touches in the Journals and Ledger

As in posting to the Profit-and-Loss Statement, when each total is posted from the journals, a checkmark (√) should be made beside the column total in the journal to show that it has been posted. Entries in the *General Ledger* should be dated as of the end of the month to which they apply. The posting reference in the *General Ledger* (column

Exhibit 10.—General Ledger Sheet

Account:			No.				
Date	Description	PR	Items posted Debit	Credit	Balance Debit	Credit

headed "PR" or "Ref.") should be "CR" for the *Cash Receipts Journal* or "CD" for the *Cash Disbursements Journal,* followed by the number of the journal page from which the item was posted.

As each entry is made in the ledger, the balances should be brought up to date. Entries should be made in ink except for the balance column. This may be kept in pencil for ease of correction in case an error is made in addition or subtraction. The balance should at all times equal the difference between the total of all postings to the debit column and the total of all postings to the credit column. It will appear in whichever column has the larger total.

Other Postings

You may have provided a separate column in your *Cash Receipts Journal* for sales taxes (which will be discussed in part 10). The total of this column should be entered in the credit column of the Sales-Tax-Payable account of the *General Ledger.* When the tax is paid, a debit entry from the *Cash Disbursements Journal* will offset the credit entry from the *Cash Receipts Journal.*

If you use an Exchange account as described in part 8, the credits recorded in the *Cash Receipts Journal* should just equal the debits recorded in the *Cash Disbursements Journal.* The account should therefore always have a zero balance and may, if you wish, be omitted from the *General Ledger.* The Exchange totals in the journals would then be marked with an "X" instead of a checkmark, to show that they are not posted.

If you are a member of a credit plan, you probably have a separate column in your *Cash Receipts Journal* for discounts on credit-plan sales. The total of this column is entered on your Profit-and-Loss Statement as an expense. It should also be posted in the *General Ledger* as a credit to Accounts Receivable. Two checkmarks should be made beside the column total to show that it has been posted twice.

Recording Ending Inventory

After all postings to the *General Ledger* have been made from the journals, an entry must be made in the Merchandise-Inventory account to record your ending inventory. There should already be a debit balance in the account equal to the beginning inventory shown on line 2 of the This-Month column of your Profit-and-Loss Statement. An entry is now made to increase or decrease this amount to the ending inventory shown on line 5 of the Profit-and-Loss Statement. The amount of the entry is the difference between the beginning and ending inventories. If the ending inventory is *larger* than the beginning inventory, the entry

Exhibit 11.—Chart of General Ledger Accounts
ASSETS
(All asset accounts normally have debit balances except those marked "CR.")

CURRENT ASSETS
- 100 Cash in bank
- 105 Petty cash
- 110 Exchange account
- 120 Accounts receivable
- 125 Allowance for bad debts *(CR.)*
- 130 Merchandise inventories

FIXED ASSETS
- 150 Land
- 160 Buildings
- 165 Allowance for depreciation—buildings *(CR.)*
- 170 Delivery equipment
- 175 Allowance for depreciation—delivery equipment *(CR.)*
- 180 Furniture and fixtures
- 185 Allowance for depreciation—furniture and fixtures *(CR.)*
- 190 Leasehold improvements
- 195 Allowance for amortization—leasehold improvements *(CR.)*

LIABILITIES [1]
(All liability accounts normally have credit balances.)

CURRENT LIABILITIES
- 200 Accounts payable
- 205 Notes payable—current
- 210 Income taxes withheld—Federal
- 215 Income taxes withheld—State
- 220 Social Security tax payable
- 225 Sales tax payable

LONG-TERM LIABILITIES
- 250 Notes payable—long term

CAPITAL [2]
(All capital accounts normally have credit balances except those marked "DR.")
- 300 Proprietor's capital
- 310 Proprietor's drawings *(DR.)*
- 350 Profit and loss *(CR. if profit; DR. if loss)*

---

[1] If the business is a corporation, the liability accounts will also include the following:
- 230 Federal income tax payable
- 235 State income tax payable

[2] The capital accounts listed here are for a single proprietorship. If the business is a partnership, capital and drawing accounts are provided for each partner. If the business is incorporated, the capital accounts are as follows:
- 300 Capital stock
- 310 Retained earnings
- 320 Dividends paid *(DR.)*
- 350 Profit and loss *(CR. if profit; DR. if loss)*

will be a *debit;* if the ending inventory is *smaller* than the beginning inventory, the entry will be a *credit.*

For example, if your beginning inventory as shown in the *General Ledger* and the Profit-and-Loss Statement is $6,000 and the ending inventory $7,500, you will make a debit entry of $1,500 in the Merchandise-Inventory account of the *General Ledger.* Since the balance of the Inventory account is always a debit balance, this entry will raise the balance to $7,500, the ending inventory figure.

If, with the same beginning inventory, your ending inventory is $5,000, you will make a credit entry of $1,000. This will reduce the $6,000 balance to $5,000.

The posting reference for this entry is "INV."

Balancing the Ledger

You are now ready to balance the *General Ledger* by adding all the debit balances and all the credit balances. The difference between these two totals should equal the net profit or loss for the month shown

---

How To Identify Errors in Computing Profit or Loss

If the difference between the debit and credit balances in the *General Ledger* does not agree with the profit or loss shown on the Profit-and-Loss statement, take the following steps to find your mistake:

• Find the amount of the difference. Is it just twice the amount of some journal posting or *General Ledger* balance? If so, that posting or balance was probably treated as a debit instead of a credit, or as a credit instead of a debit.

• Check the additions of the Profit-and-Loss Statement and of the *General Ledger* balances.

• Check both journals to see that all items that should have been posted to either the Profit-and-Loss Statement or the *General Ledger* were correctly posted.

• Check each journal to see that the total of all debit items posted equals the total of all credit items posted.

• Check to see that the beginning-of-the-month and end-of-the-month balances of the Merchandise Inventory account in the *General Ledger* agree with the same items on the Profit-and-Loss Statement.

• Check the *General Ledger* to see (a) that the debit balances equaled the credit balances *before* this month's postings; and (b) that the balance in the Profit-and-Loss account agrees with the year-to-date profit or loss figure on the preceding month's Profit-and-Loss Statement.

68

Exhibit 12

ABC STORE

Balance Sheet, _____, 19—

Assets

Current assets:
  Cash:
    Cash in bank................ $_____
    Petty cash.................. _____ $_____
  Accounts receivable.............. $_____
    Less allowance for doubtful accounts..................... _____   _____
  Merchandise inventories.......... _____
    Total current assets............ $_____
Fixed assets:
  Land.......................... $_____
  Buildings...................... _____
  Delivery equipment.............. _____
  Furniture and fixtures........... _____ $_____
    Less allowance for depreciation... _____
       $_____
  Leasehold improvements, less amortization................ _____
    Total fixed assets.............. _____
Total assets....................... $_____

Liabilities and Capital [1]

Current liabilities:
  Accounts payable................ $_____
  Notes payable, due within 1 year... _____
  Payroll taxes and withheld taxes.... _____
  Sales taxes...................... _____
    Total current liabilities......... $_____
Long-term liabilities:
  Notes payable, due after 1 year..... _____
Total liabilities.................... $_____
Capital:
  Proprietor's capital, beginning of period..................... $_____
  Net profit for the period.......... $_____
  Less proprietor's drawings [2]........ _____
  Increase in capital............... _____
    Capital, end of period.......... _____
Total liabilities and capital........... $_____

[1] For partnership or corporation, see footnotes to exhibit 11.

[2] If the business suffers a loss, the proprietor's drawings will be *added* to the net loss to give the total *decrease* in capital.

on your Profit-and-Loss Statement. If the debits total more than the credits, your business has made a profit; if the credits total more than the debits, it has suffered a loss.

If the profit or loss shown by the totals of the *General Ledger* balances equals that shown on your Profit-and-Loss Statement, this amount is posted to the Profit-and-Loss account in your *General Ledger*—as a credit if it represents a profit; as a debit if it represents a loss. The debits and credits in the ledger should now balance.

But what if, when you compare the difference between the debit and credit balances in the *General Ledger* with the month's profit or loss as shown by the Profit-and-Loss Statement, the two figures do not agree? There are only a few areas where an error could have been made. Follow the steps listed in the box on page 67 to identify the mistake before you post the profit or loss to the *General Ledger*.

Preparing the Monthly Balance Sheet

A balance sheet is a summary of the *General Ledger* accounts. In contrast to the Profit-and-Loss Statement, which covers an entire accounting period, the balance sheet is for a specific date. Therefore, it does not have "this month" and "year to date" figures. It is usually desirable, however, to show the balances as of the same date in the current year and in the preceding year.

An example of a balance sheet for a single proprietorship is shown as exhibit 12. It simply lists the acounts as they appear in the *General Ledger,* with their balances and with the additions and subtractions necessary to show the total assets, liabilities, and capital. (This example shows only the current year.) Remember that "the balance sheet must balance"; that is, total assets must equal total liabilities plus capital.

Steps To Be Taken at the End of the Year

The basic unit of time for both accounting and tax purposes is a year. In many cases, this is a calendar year ending December 31, but it may be a fiscal year ending with the last day of any month. There may be advantages in adopting a fiscal year other than the calendar year if (1) your business is seasonal and inventories and accounts receivable are lower at a time of the year other than December 31, or (2) the demands of your business in the spring make it hard for you to find time to prepare a tax return.

Clearing Away the Deadwood

Whether your accounting is done on a fiscal-year or calendar-year basis, steps must be taken at the end of the year to *close your books*.

1. Bring your depreciation schedules up to date as described in part 9. Normally, your depreciation entry in the *Cash Disbursements Journal* for the last month of the year will bring your books into agreement with your depreciation schedules.

2. Review your accounts receivable with the thought of charging off all bad debts and any longstanding differences between your detailed records and the *General Ledger* account. Also review your allowance for bad debts and make any adjustments needed. (See part 7.)

3. Review your inventory valuation to make sure that no unsalable or slow-moving merchandise is being carried at too high a value.

4. Review your bank reconciliation and consider writing off any checks that have been outstanding for a long time (at least a year). To write off a check, make an entry in the *Cash Disbursements Journal* reversing the entry made when the check was drawn. The amount of the check is entered as a deduction (circled or in red) in the Amount-of-Check column and as a credit under Miscellaneous Income and Expense Items, with the account listed as "Other income." The amount is also added to the balance in your checkbook.

These steps should be taken *before you prepare your financial statements for the last month of your accounting year*. The year-to-date profit or loss shown on the final statements will be the figure you use for tax-return purposes.

If your business is a corporation, the final tax liability should also be computed so that it can be included in your statements. If you cannot compute the exact tax liability before closing your books, the closest possible estimate should be made. Any minor difference between the estimated tax recorded for the year and the final tax paid can be added to or deducted from the next year's income tax on your statements. A large difference, however, should appear on your next year's Profit-and-Loss Statement as "Overestimate (or Underestimate) of last year's taxes."

Closing the Profit-and-Loss and Proprietor's-Drawings Accounts

After the steps listed above have been completed, the Profit-and-Loss account and the Proprietor's-Drawings account in the *General Ledger* are *closed into* the Proprietor's-Capital account. No entries are needed in the journals.

For a sole proprietorship, the closing entries in the *General Ledger* are as follows:

1. If you have a profit, the amount of the profit is entered as a debit in the Profit-and-Loss account and as a credit in the Proprietor's-Capital account.

2. If you have a loss, the Profit-and-Loss account is credited and the Proprietor's-Capital account debited for the amount of the loss.

3. The total of the Proprietor's-Drawings account is then credited to that account and debited to the Proprietor's-Capital account.

These entries reduce the Profit-and-Loss and Proprietor's-Drawings accounts to zero.

If your business is a partnership, each partner's drawings account is closed into his capital account and the profit or loss distributed to the capital accounts. Just how this is done depends on the partnership agreement.

If your business is a corporation, the Profit-and-Loss account is closed into the Retained-Earnings account. The Dividends-Paid account is closed by crediting that account and debiting the Retained-Earnings account for the amount of the dividends paids. This entry reduces the Dividends-Paid account to zero.

The Final Balance

After these closing entries have been made, your *General Ledger* should still be in balance—that is, the sum of the credit balances should equal the sum of the debit balances. Some business owners prefer to start a new year by bringing forward, or transferring to new ledger sheets, all the *General Ledger* account balances, but this is not necessary. If it is done, the new ledger sheets should be checked to make certain that the total of the debit balances still equals the total of the credit balances. This will show up any errors that may have been made in copying the balances onto the new sheets.

| Part 7 | The Absentee Asset: Accounts Receivable |

Recording Accounts Receivable......................... 75

    The Accounts Receivable Ledger.......................... 75

    The Accounts Receivable Control Sheet................... 75

    Billing Customers.. 77

    Unidentified Items...................................... 79

    Credit Plans... 80

Aging Your Accounts Receivable...................... 81

Accounting for Bad Debts............................. 82

    The Direct Charge-off Method........................... 82

    The Allowance Method................................. 83

    Payments Received on Bad Debts....................... 84

Recording
Accounts Receivable

If you extend credit to your customers, you must keep an accurate account of the amount each customer owes you and be systematic about billing and collections. This is important. It results in better relations with your credit customers and in fewer losses from bad debts.

The Accounts Receivable Ledger

The simplest method of handling accounts receivable—other than just keeping a file of sales-slip carbons—is to have a ledger sheet, or account, for each credit customer. These accounts are kept in an *Accounts Receivable Ledger* in alphabetical order. After the *Daily Summary of Sales and Cash Receipts* has been completed, the charge-sales checks and cash-receipt slips for payments on account are arranged in alphabetical order and posted to the individual customers' accounts in the ledger.

Exhibit 13 shows a typical accounts-receivable ledger sheet. For each credit sale, the entry should show the date, the sales-check number, and the amount of the sale, which is recorded in the debit column. Returned sales are also recorded in the debit column, but as a deduction (that is, in red or circled). Collections on account are entered in the credit column. After each entry, the new balance should be computed by adding sales to the previous balance or deducting cash receipts and returns.

The Accounts Receivable Control Sheet

In addition to the individual customer accounts, a control sheet should be set up. The same form is used for the control sheet as for the individual accounts. The total Charges to Customers and total Collections on Account are entered on this sheet from the *Daily Summary*—charges

Exhibit 13.—Accounts Receivable Ledger: Customer's Account

John Doe 345 Sixth Street					
Date		**Item**	**Debit**	**Credit**	**Balance**
Sep	1	Balance			47 62
	8	Sales check #195	4 50		52 12
	10	Received on account		47 62	4 50
	19	Sales check #231	42 50		47 00
	20	Sales check #243, return sale	(35 00)		12 00

Exhibit 14.—Accounts Receivable Ledger: Control Sheet

Accounts Receivable Control Sheet					
Date		**Item**	**Debit**	**Credit**	**Balance**
Nov	1	Balance brought forward			2395 00
	1		80 00		2475 00
	2		230 00	195 00	2510 00

in the debit column and collections in the credit column. A running balance is maintained as for the individual customers' accounts. (See exhibit 14.)

At any time, the balance on the control sheet should equal the total of the balances of all the individual accounts. If it does not, follow the procedure outlined in the box on page 78. When you first set up your records and whenever you assign your recordkeeping to a new person, it is best to check the balances after each day's posting. Later, as the daily balancing and posting become routine, the check may be made weekly, and then, if no problems occur, only at the end of the month.

This check shows whether your accounts are mathematically correct, but it does not show whether any postings have been made to the wrong customer's account. This problem, and the resulting harm to your customer relations, can only be avoided through care on the part of the person keeping your records or by having the work reviewed by another person.

If you are able to balance your accounts receivable each month without difficulty, you can do away with the accounts-receivable control sheet and balance your accounts directly to the *General Ledger* Accounts-Receivable account. In any case, the balance on the control sheet in the *Accounts Receivable Ledger* should agree with the balance of the *General Ledger* Accounts-Receivable account at the end of each month.

When the day's posting has been finished, the sales checks and cash-receipts tickets should be filed by dates.

Billing Customers

At the end of each month, a statement should be sent to each of your customers whose account has a balance. You may have your statement forms printed so as to show the name, address, and telephone number of your business. However, standard statement forms can be bought, and you can write, type, or stamp the information on them.

Each customer's statement is essentially a copy of his ledger sheet for that month. The beginning balance, sales, returns, cash payments, and ending balance are shown. A carbon copy of the statement should be made for your records.

A timesaver. If your business has a number of credit transactions with each customer, you may be able to save bookkeeping time by accumulating each customer's sales checks and receipts in a jacket or pocket during the month instead of posting them. At the end of the month, the sales checks can be added and the adding machine tape or penciled addition stapled to them and enclosed with a statement showing only the customer's balance at the end of the month. This one total is also entered on the customer's ledger sheet.

A record of some sort must be made of the details of the sales billed, however. This can be done by running a second adding machine tape of the sales checks, recording on it the sales-check number applying to each amount, and retaining it in your files. (This will also check the addition on the statement sent to the customer.) Another method is to note each sales-check number in the description column of the customer's ledger sheet. Still another is to list each sales-check number and amount on the statement instead of enclosing the sales checks and adding-machine tape or penciled addition. With a small number of transactions, the sales-check number should make it possible for you to find the sales check if any question comes up after you have billed the customer.

Before you mail the statement. Before the statements are put in the envelopes for mailing, the ending balances shown on all statements should be totaled to make sure that the total of these balances agrees with the

How To Handle Errors in Accounts Receivable Balances

If your *Accounts Receivable Ledger* does not balance after a day's posting, total all sales posted to the customers' accounts for the day. The result should agree with the charge sales reported on the *Daily Summary*. If it does not, the difference might be due to one of the following causes:

• Incorrect amount posted to a customer's account.
• Amount posted to a customer's account incorrectly added or subtracted.
• Charge sales incorrectly totaled for the *Daily Summary*.
• Sales check missing.

Any of these errors could be located by comparing the adding-machine tape or penciled addition of the ledger postings with the additions of charge sales for the *Daily Summary*. Collections on account should be checked in the same way.

If, after any necessary corrections, the sales and cash postings agree with the *Daily Summary* but the total of the individual ledger accounts still does not agree with the control sheet, look for an error in addition on the customers' ledger sheets or the control sheet.

If the source of a discrepancy cannot be located, note the amount of the difference on the control sheet. The next time you try to balance these accounts, you may find that they still differ by the same amount. This will mean that no further error has been made. At the end of the year, differences still unsolved should be charged off by using the method described below for writing off bad debts.

balance shown on the accounts-receivable control sheet. This can take the place of the end-of-the-month balancing of the *Accounts Receivable Ledger* already described. It will check, not only the accuracy of the *Accounts Receivable Ledger,* but also the accuracy of the copying of the statements.

As the statements are being prepared, all customers having unpaid balances from the preceding month should be noted. A reminder of the overdue balance should be enclosed with the statements of these customers.

Unidentified Items

In part 2 it was mentioned that you may occasionally have collections on account that cannot be identified because of missing or incomplete information. The *Accounts Receivable Ledger* should include a sheet headed "Unidentified Cash" to which each of these items is posted. This ledger sheet is handled like a customer's account in balancing, except that it always has a credit balance.

Recording unidentified payments. The customers involved will probably call your attention to the fact that they have not been given credit for these payments. If a payment claimed by a customer can be identified as having been entered in the unidentified-cash account, the amount is entered as a credit in the customer's account and as a debit in the Unidentified-Cash account. It does not have to be entered in your journals nor on your accounts-receivable control sheet, but an explanation should be noted in both the customer's account and the Unidentified-Cash account.

Recording unidentified charge sales. Occasionally there may be a charge-sales check on which the salesperson neglected to enter the customer's name. If the salesperson cannot remember what customer it was, the sales check should be posted as a debit to an account headed "Unidentified Customers." It is much less likely that a customer will call your attention to a missing charge than to a missing payment, but there is a possibility that the sale might later be identified. If this happens, the customer's account is debited and the Unidentified-Customers account credited for the amount.

Charging off unidentified items. At the end of the year, you should review the Unidentified-Cash and Unidentified-Customers account and charge off old balances that it appears will never be identified. The method for doing this is described later in the discussion of writing off bad debts.

Credit Plans

In many localities, there are central credit plans or services. There are also several well-known national credit-card organizations that operate in much the same manner as the local plans.

Under a typical credit plan, your customer has a card allowing him to deal on a credit basis with you and many other merchants in your area. You submit all sales checks from such customers to the plan at agreed-upon intervals and receive a check for the total amount less a service charge. The billing and collection functions are then taken over by the credit plan.

The plan will probably furnish you standard transmittal envelopes in which to remit your sales checks. (Unless you have a very small volume of sales, daily remittances are advisable.) The transmittal envelopes will probably provide a tally on which to total the enclosed sales checks and a space for computing the discount or service charge and showing the net amount you will receive from the plan.

Recording credit-plan sales. If you are a member of a credit plan, you will not need a separate *Accounts Receivable Ledger,* since you will have only one account—an account for the plan. (If you are a member of two or more plans, of course, an account will be needed for each plan.)

As with noncredit-plan charge sales, the total of the day's charge sales is entered on the *Daily Summary* and from there to the *Sales and Cash Receipts Journal.* As each transmittal is prepared, the total of the charge sales included is posted as a debit on the Accounts-Receivable ledger sheet. The service charge can be recorded in a column added to the *Sales and Cash Receipts Journal.* This column will not enter into the previously described cross-checking of the journal columns; but at the end of the month, the total of the column will be posted as a credit to the Accounts-Receivable account and as an expense item on the Profit-and-Loss Statement.

Payments received from the plan are recorded in the *Daily Summary* and *Cash Receipts Journal* like any other collection on account and posted to the credit column of the Accounts-Receivable ledger sheet. If a transmittal slip is corrected by the plan and as a result the amount received is not the amount you computed and entered in your records, a correcting entry should be made in the columns involved.

After all posting has been completed, the balance due from the credit plan as shown in the Accounts-Receivable account should equal the net amount of all transmittals for which payment has not been received.

Aging Your Accounts Receivable

At least two or three times a year, your accounts receivable should be *aged*. To do this, make up a sheet with the following column headings: "Total Amount," "Current," "30–60 Days," "60–90 days," "3–6 Months," "6–9 Months," "9–12 Months," and "Over 1 Year" (see exhibit 15).

The balance of each of your accounts receivable is then entered in the Total-Amount column. If all the charges in a given account were made in the current month, the total is also entered in the Current column. If the charges made in the current month do not account for the entire balance, enough of the charges made in the preceding month are entered in the 30–60 Days column to make up the difference. If no charges were made in the preceding month, or if the charges made then are not enough to make up the difference, the charges for the next preceding month—or enough to make up the total—are entered in the 60–90 Days column; and so on. If no charge sales were made to the customer in the time period covered by any of the columns, no entry is made in that column, even though entries may be necessary in earlier columns.

Suppose that customer A (exhibit 15) has a balance of $103.50 on September 30. Following is a summary of his account for the past 4 months:

	Debit	Credit	Balance
June	51.50	. . . . . .	51.50
July	. . . . . .	50.00	1.50
August. .	49.50	. . . . . .	51.00
September.	52.50	. . . . . .	103.50

On the aging schedule, his balance of $103.50 is entered in the Total-Amount column and his September purchases of $52.50 in the Current column. Since all of his August purchases are needed to make up the balance, the $49.50 is entered in the 30–60 Days column. $1.50 of the total balance is still to be accounted for. He made no purchases on account during July, however; so no entry is made in the 60–90 Days column. Instead, the $1.50 is entered in the 3–6 Months column, since the $1.50 is a part of the June charges.

After all the individual accounts have been aged, each column should be totaled. The total of the Total-Amount column should equal the sum of the totals of the other columns. It should also agree with the total in the accounts-receivable control sheet.

Aging your accounts receivable brings to your attention accounts that are slow and deserve extra collection effort or suspension of credit privileges. It is also useful in comparing the overall aging of your accounts receivable for different periods. For this purpose, the percentages of the total represented by the individual columns are more useful than the dollar amounts.

Exhibit 15.—Aging of Accounts Receivable

Customer	Total Amount	Current	30–60 Days	60–90 Days	3–6 Months	6–9 Months	9–12 Months	Over 1 Year
A	$103.50	$52.50	$49.50		$1.50			
B	23.00	23.00						
C	9.75					$5.50	$4.25	
M	4.25	4.25						
N	45.00	29.75	15.25					
O	12.00	7.00		$5.00				
R	10.00							$10.00
S	50.00	50.00						
X	28.00	20.00	8.00					
Y	14.50				14.50			
Z	35.00	35.00						
Total	$450.00	$336.50	$72.75	$5.00	$16.00	$5.50	$4.25	$10.00
Percent	100	75	16	1	4	1	1	2

Accounting for Bad Debts

Any business that grants credit will sooner or later run into collection losses, or "bad debts." Such losses may be recorded in either of two ways: by the direct charge-off method, or by the allowance method.

The Direct Charge-off Method

Under this method, when it becomes obvious that one or more accounts are uncollectible (usually determined by a periodic review of your customers' accounts), they are removed from the books, or "charged off," as follows:

1. The total of all the balances to be charged off is entered in the *Cash Disbursements, Purchases, and Expense Journal*—as a debit under Miscellaneous Income and Expense Items with the description "Bad Debts," and as a credit under General Ledger Items, with "Accounts Receivable" shown as the account.

2. The total is also entered in the credit column of the accounts-receivable control sheet to reduce the accounts-receivable balance by that amount.

3. The individual amounts are entered in the credit columns of the individual customer accounts. This will ordinarily reduce each of the accounts involved to zero.

Any long-standing difference between the total of the individual customer accounts and the control sheet (discussed on page 75) should be included in the bad-debts total entered in the journal and on the control sheet. No individual customer account is affected by this adjustment

The Allowance Method

Under the allowance method of accounting for bad-debt losses, it is assumed that some accounts will prove uncollectible. An allowance is therefore provided against which the bad accounts can be charged.

Setting up the allowance. The first problem is to know how much of an allowance to provide. If you have a going business, your past bad-debt losses will serve as a guide; but if you are just starting in business, you will have to make an estimate. Bad-debt losses vary greatly with type of business, credit and collection policies, and the economic environment in which your business operates. Your best guide to the bad debts to be expected is the experience of other businesses as similar to yours as possible.   You may be able to get this information from a trade association, your suppliers, or personal acquaintances in your type of business.

After you have decided on the rate of provision for bad debts, an entry is made at the end of each month in the *Cash Disbursements, Purchases, and Expense Journal*.   The description is entered as "Bad Debts" and the amount of the monthly allowance is entered as a debit under Miscellaneous Income and Expense Items and as a credit under General Ledger Items.   The *General Ledger* entry will be posted to the account "Allowance for Bad Debts."

Periodically, but in any case at the end of each year, you should measure your allowance for bad debts against an aging of your accounts receivable.   If you feel that the allowance is not large enough, an additional entry to make up the amount needed should be made; if you feel that it is already too large, an entry reversing a part of the allowance previously provided should be made.   This analysis will also suggest whether you should raise or lower the monthly "bad debts" entry for future periods.

Charging off the bad debts.   Your customer accounts should be reviewed periodically to determine which ones should be charged off. The total of these uncollectible accounts is then entered in the *Cash Disbursements Journal* under General Ledger Items—once as a debit with the account described as "Allowance for bad debts" and again as a credit with the account described as "Accounts receivable."   The total is also entered in the credit column of the accounts-receivable control sheet, and the individual amounts are entered in the credit columns of the individual customer accounts.

Payments Received on Bad Debts

Occasionally, a collection may be received on an account after the account has been charged off as uncollectible.   Such a receipt is recorded in the *Daily Summary* and in the *Cash Receipts Journal,* but not as cash received on account, since the account is no longer on the books.   The entry is included in the miscellaneous receipts on the *Daily Summary* and is entered in the *Cash Receipts Journal* as a credit under General Ledger Items, with the account shown as "Allowance for Bad Debts."   It will, of course, be in the Total Cash Deposit.

It is possible that at the time the cash receipt is recorded, the person recording it will not realize that the account has been charged off and will record the receipt as a normal collection on account.   The error will be discovered when the entry is to be posted to the customer's account. At that time, a correcting entry is made.   The amount of the cash receipt is entered as a credit under General Ledger Items, with the account shown as "Allowance for bad debts," and as a deduction in the Collections-on-Account column.

Part 8 | Some Special Cash Receipts Situations

Return Sales and Refunds................................ 87

    Types of Refunds...................................... 87

    Returns or Refunds on Charge Sales..................... 88

    Returns or Refunds on Cash Sales...................... 88

    Refunds for Returnable Containers...................... 89

Making Purchases from Cash Receipts.................. 89

Cashing Customers' Checks............................. 90

    Handling Bad Checks................................... 91

    When Many Checks Are Cashed.......................... 91

Redeeming Coupons..................................... 94

    Recording the Coupons................................ 95

    When the Amounts Are Very Small...................... 95

Return Sales and Refunds

In most businesses, it is sometimes necessary to accept returned merchandise for credit or refund. In some cases, refunds are made without the return of merchandise.

You should establish certain safeguards to protect yourself against unauthorized returns, returns of merchandise purchased elsewhere, or refund or credit of too great an amount. These safeguards should include the following policy rules:

1. The original cash-register slip or sales check must be presented when merchandise is returned.

2. No refunds will be made on purchases after a specified length of time.

3. No cash refunds will be made on charge purchases.

4. All returns must be made at a designated place in the store or be approved by one or more authorized persons.

Types of Refunds

Refunds will generally be necessary because of one of the following situations:

Return of resalable merchandise.
Return of defective or unsalable merchandise.
Refund of overcharge.
Refund for adjustment on unsatisfactory merchandise kept by customer.
Refund of deposit on returnable containers (soft-drink bottles and so on).

When salable merchandise is returned, it should be returned to stock promptly. When unsalable or defective merchandise is returned or a customer is given an adjustment for unsatisfactory merchandise, determine whether the supplier should be held responsible for the defect. If so, take steps to recover your purchase price or the amount of the adjustment from him.

An even exchange in which the return merchandise is salable and the replacing merchandise comes from the same department need not be recorded. Uneven exchanges and even exchanges in which the replacing merchandise is from a different department should be treated as returns of the old items and new sales of the replacing items.

Returns or Refunds on Charge Sales

In any type of return or refund on a charge sale, a credit slip should be issued to the customer. This can be a regular sales check plainly marked "return sale" or "credit." Or, if you have enough returns to justify it, you can use special credit slips. If special credit slips are used, they should be prenumbered and controlled in the same way that charge-sales checks are.

When you add up the charge sales for the *Daily Summary,* any sales checks representing returns or refunds on charge sales are subtracted from the total. The net charge-sales figure is then entered on the summary. The return or refund sales checks should be kept with the rest of the day's charge-sales checks to be entered as credits to the individual customer accounts.

Returns or Refunds on Cash Sales

There are several methods of handling returns on merchandise for which the customer paid cash.

1. If you use sales checks instead of a cash register, a credit sales check marked "cash refund" should be made out and the cash refunded to the customer. Information taken from the original sales check should be entered on the credit slip so that the amount of the credit can be deducted from the totals of the proper department. When the cash-sales figure is prepared for the *Daily Summary,* the amount of the refund will be subtracted from the total.

2. If you use a cash register with a return-sales key, the return sale is rung up. Some cash registers subtract return sales directly from sales. In such cases, the totals in the cash register at the end of the day are net sales and can be entered on the *Daily Summary* as they are. Other cash registers show only the total returned sales, and this total must be subtracted from the cash-sales total.

3. If you do not have many return sales and refunds and they do not add up to much money, they can be treated as petty-cash payments and a petty-cash slip made out for them.

4. For large refunds, you may not want to make a cash refund from the cash register. In that case, you can issue a check to the customer for

the amount of the refund. The check does not affect the *Daily Summary*—sales will be reduced when the check is recorded in the *Cash Disbursements Journal*.

Refunds for Returnable Containers

Refunds of deposits on soft-drink bottles or other returnable containers are routine and usually small. They should be handled with as little recordkeeping as possible.

One way to do this is to have a special place where all such bottles or containers are to be returned. A clerk stationed nearby is given a fund large enough to take care of a normal day's refunds. In smaller stores, the bottle fund may be simply set aside in a small container.

When bottles are returned, the customer is paid, and no record is made of the payment. At the end of the day, the bottles are sorted by type and their total deposit value computed. This amount plus the remaining cash should equal the fixed amount of the fund. A memo of the total day's refunds is then given to the main cashier, who restores that amount to the "bottle fund." Since the deposit, when it was collected, was treated as part of the sales price, the total of the deposits refunded during the day is deducted from the cash-sales total when the *Daily Summary* is prepared. The memo is kept with the summary.

Making Purchases from Cash Receipts

It is important that you (1) deposit all cash receipts, (2) make all major payments of the business by check, and (3) handle all other cash payments through a petty-cash fund. Sometimes, however, exceptions must be made to these rules. In some types of business—particularly groceries or rural general stores—it is customary to make many merchandise purchases for cash rather than by check. These purchases may be from suppliers' route men or from farmers. If your volume of such purchases is substantial, you will not find it practical to handle them through your petty-cash fund.

The following suggestions will help to keep your records in good shape if you must make payments from cash receipts:

1. Try to confine all such payments to one type of spending (for example, merchandise purchases) and use the petty-cash fund for all other cash payments.

2. Always get a written receipt showing vendor's name, date, a brief description of the purchase, and the amount paid.

3. If you use a cash register, have a paid-out key and ring up each payment made from cash receipts. At the end of each day, balance the total from the paid-out register against the total of the written receipts for the day's cash purchases. If you do not use a cash register, or if your cash register does not have a paid-out key, the receipts can be added to get the total paid-outs for the day.

4. Design your *Daily Summary* so that item 4, "Total receipts to be accounted for" is a subtotal. From this figure deduct the total of your day's paid-outs to get "Net receipts to be accounted for." The "Cash Receipts" section of the *Daily Summary* will then read as follows (the rest of the form will be as shown in exhibit 3):

```
Cash sales_____  $_____
Collections on account_____     _____
Miscellaneous receipts_____     _____
Total receipts_____  $_____
Less merchandise purchases_____     _____
NET RECEIPTS TO BE ACCOUNTED FOR___  $=======
```

5. Design your *Sales and Cash Receipts Journal* (exhibit 4) to conform to the *Daily Summary*. That is, provide an additional column headed "Merchandise Purchases." This column will be a debit column. The total must be included in the amount entered for purchases on the Profit-and-Loss Statement.

Cashing Customers' Checks

In some communities and in some types of business, checks are often cashed for quite a number of customers. To protect yourself, you should take the following precautions before accepting checks:

1. If the check is a personal check, know the person who wrote it (or the endorser presenting the check) and be reasonably certain that he is good for the amount of the check. In effect, you are extending credit to him until the check clears the bank.

2. In the case of payroll checks, know the company and require the endorser presenting the check to identify himself as the payee.

3. Get enough information from the one presenting the check to enable you to contact him if you need to.

Handling "Bad Checks"

In spite of precautions, in almost any business where checks are taken from customers, now and then a check will be returned by the bank as uncollectible. When this happens, contact the person from whom you accepted the check at once. Try to get him to replace it with cash or another check. If the check is made good in the same month, no entry is needed in your *Daily Summary* or in the *Sales and Cash Receipts Journal*. However, a new deposit slip should be prepared and your copy marked, "Replacement of *(customer's name)* check returned by bank on *(date)*."

If a returned check has not been made good by the end of the month in which it was returned, an entry should be made in your checkbook to reduce your bank balance by the amount of the check. An entry is also needed in the *Sales and Cash Receipts Journal,* as follows:

1. Write the name of the customer and "Returned check" in the description column.

2. Enter the amount of the check, in red or circled to show that it is a deduction, under Total Cash Deposit.

3. If the check was originally received as a payment on account, enter the amount, in red or circled, under Collections on Account.

4. If the check was for any other purpose, enter it in the debit column under Miscellaneous Income and Expense Items, with the account described as "Bad check."

You should go on trying to collect the check. If you succeed in collecting it in a later month, the collection is recorded among the cash receipts on the *Daily Summary*—as a collection on account if the original check was a payment on account; otherwise, as a miscellaneous receipt to be entered in the *Sales and Cash Receipts Journal* as a credit under Miscellaneous Income and Expense Items. In other words, the entries made at the time the new check is deposited reverse the entries made when the check was returned.

When Many Checks Are Cashed

Some businesses cash so many checks for customers that the money taken in from other customers is not enough to take care of the check cashing. As a result, the change fund has to be larger than would otherwise be necessary.

Exhibit 16.—Daily Summary of Sales and Cash Receipts With Excess Checks Entry

DAILY SUMMARY OF SALES AND CASH RECEIPTS

Date March 23, 19—

CASH RECEIPTS

1.	Cash sales...............................	$435.00
2.	Collections on account......................	100.00
3.	Miscellaneous receipts [1]...................	15.00
4.	TOTAL RECEIPTS TO BE ACCOUNTED FOR.	$550.00

CASH ON HAND

5. Cash in register or till:

Coins........................	$ 25.00	
Bills............................	43.00	
Checks........................	562.00	
Total cash in register or till................		$630.00

6.	Petty-cash slips.............................	14.00
7.	TOTAL CASH ACCOUNTED FOR...........	$644.00

8. Less change and petty-cash fund:

Petty-cash slips....................	$14.00	
Coins and bills....................	86.00	
Change and petty-cash fund (fixed amount)..		100.00

9.	Receipts to be deposited......................	544.00
9a.	Excess checks to be deposited.................	18.00
9b.	TOTAL CASH DEPOSIT...................	$562.00
10.	CASH SHORT (Item 4 less item 9 if item 4 is larger).	$ 6.00
11.	CASH OVER (Item 9 less item 4 if item 9 is larger).	$ ——

TOTAL SALES

12.	Cash sales................................	$435.00
13.	Charge sales (saleschecks #262, to #316)..........	225.00
14.	TOTAL SALES............................	$660.00

By John Doe

[1] Note to appear on back of summary: "Miscellaneous receipts: Refund on merchandise $15.00."

In such circumstances, so many checks may be cashed for customers that the coins and bills at the end of the day are not enough to bring the change fund up to the fixed amount for the next day. If this happens in your business, all the checks should be deposited, but to do this and at the same time restore the change fund to its fixed amount will require some changes in your bookkeeping setup.

Changes in the Daily Summary form. Your *Daily Summary* form will have to be a little different from the one shown in exhibit 3. You will need to make the following changes in the form:

Change the wording of item 9, "Total cash deposit," to "Receipts to be deposited." *This is still the item that should equal item 4, "Total receipts to be accounted for," and on which cash short or over will be based.*

Add item 9a, "Excess checks or cash [1] to be deposited."
Add item 9b, "Total cash deposit."

Item 9a will be the amount by which the checks (shown in item 5) exceed the receipts to be deposited (item 9). Item 9b will be the sum of items 9 and 9a and should be the same as the amount of the checks (item 5). On days when the receipts to be deposited total more than the checks cashed, item 9a will not be used, and item 9b will be the same as item 9.

Changes in the Cash Receipts Journal. When you enter the *Daily Summary* in the *Sales and Cash Receipts Journal*, item 9b is entered under Total Cash Deposit. An additional credit column headed "Exchange" is provided, and the amount of the excess checks entered there. If the checks cashed for customers exceed the receipts to be deposited on only 1 or 2 days a month, a credit entry in the General-Ledger column with "Exchange" written in the description column, can be used instead of an additional column.

Exhibit 16 shows how your *Daily Summary* will look if the checks you cash for customers total more than the day's total receipts. Illustration II on exhibit 4 (page 26) shows the journal entries for this summary. The check to restore the change fund (see below) will be drawn for $18.00 in the illustration.

Restoring the change fund. To restore the change fund, when you deposit the checks, cash at the bank a check drawn on your own account to "Petty Cash" for the amount of the *excess* checks. The money is put into the change fund to bring the fund up to its fixed amount. The check will be entered in the General-Ledger debit column of the *Cash*

---

[1] There may be excess cash to deposit if the change fund is being reduced. This will be explained later (see p. 94).

Disbursements Journal with the account shown as "Exchange." This entry will cancel the Exchange entry made in the *Cash Receipts Journal.*

Increasing and decreasing the change fund. There may be only a few days each month when, because of paydays at large companies in your locality, you expect to do a large amount of check cashing for your customers. If that is the case, you do not need to carry the larger change fund all the time. You can increase the fund temporarily by drawing a "Petty Cash" check for the amount of the increase and cashing it at the bank on the day you expect to need a larger change fund. This check will be entered in the *Cash Disbursements Journal* as a debit under General Ledger Items, with the account shown as "Exchange." Be careful, while the fund is increased, to take the proper amount of the fund into account in balancing the day's cash.

When you no longer need the extra cash, you can return the fund to its normal amount as follows:

1. If the excess checks you would otherwise enter as item 9a are *less* than the temporary increase in the fund, enter the amount of the temporary increase as item 9a, instead of the amount of the excess checks.

2. If the excess checks entered as item 9a total *more* than the temporary increase in the fund, reduce the Petty Cash check drawn for that day by the amount of the temporary increase in the fund.

In either case, follow the instructions in part 3 for entering the *Daily Summary* and the "Petty Cash" check in the journals. This will result in credits and debits to Exchange that will exactly offset the entry in the *Cash Disbursements Journal* made when the check to increase the fund was drawn.

Redeeming Coupons

More and more often, manufacturers are offering coupons that can be used as part payment on certain products. The merchant who redeems the coupons sends them to the manufacturer or his representative and receives cash for them in the amount of the coupons, usually plus a certain amount for the trouble of handling them.

If you redeem many of these coupons, they should be treated like cash when they are received from the customer. The entire amount of the sale is recorded or rung up and the coupons put in the cash register or till, along with the actual money paid by the customer.

Recording the Coupons

When you balance the day's work, these coupons are treated as petty-cash slips and are included in the amount entered on the *Daily Summary* for petty-cash slips. They can be included in the "Petty Cash" check used to restore the fund, or a special check can be made for the amount of the coupons alone. In either case, when the check is drawn, the coupons are sent to the manufacturer (or manufacturers), and the amount of the coupons is recorded as an account receivable.

A short letter should be sent with the coupons stating the number and type of coupons enclosed, their total face value, and the total amount due you, including the handling charges. A carbon copy of the letter should be kept in case you need to follow up on it.

When you receive the check from the manufacturer, the face value of the coupons is recorded as a collection on account. The handling charges are treated as a miscellaneous receipt on the *Daily Summary* and entered in the *Sales and Cash Receipts Journal* as a credit under Miscellaneous Income and Expense Items.

When the Amounts Are Very Small

If the coupons sent to any one manufacturer represent a very small amount, some recordkeeping can be avoided by making out a petty-cash slip for the coupons at the time they are sent to the manufacturer. This petty-cash slip is left in the petty-cash fund until the check is received from the manufacturer. It is not included in any checks written in the meantime to restore the fund.

When the check is received, only the handling charge is recorded. The petty-cash slip is destroyed, since it is offset by the balance of the check from the manufacturer. In effect, the petty-cash slip is like an I O U from the manufacturer for the time it remains in the petty-cash fund.

Part 9

Depreciation and Disposal of Plant Assets

Computing Depreciation of Property and Equipment .. 99

Factors in Computing Depreciation........................ 99

The Straight-Line Method of Depreciation................. 99

Other Depreciation Methods............................. 100

Sum-of-the-Years-Digits Method......................... 100

Double-Declining-Balance Method........................ 101

Amortizing Leasehold Improvements..................... 102

Recording the Purchase and Depreciation of Plant Assets. 102

Recording the Purchase................................. 102

Depreciation Schedules................................. 103

Recording the Depreciation in Your Books................ 106

Recording the Sale, Trade-in, or Junking of Plant Assets. 107

Sale of a Fully Depreciated Asset........................ 109

Sale of an Asset with Book Value........................ 109

Trade-in of an Asset.................................... 109

Junking of an Asset.................................... 110

Recording Disposal of Property on the Depreciation Schedule.. 111

Computing Depreciation
of Property and Equipment

Whatever type of business you are in, you will have to purchase property and equipment from time to time. This property will usually last for several years, so it would not be realistic to consider the whole cost an expense in any one year. Therefore, when the property is purchased, it is set upon the books as a *fixed,* or *plant, asset.* The decrease in value over the life of the property, known as depreciation, is treated as an expense distributed over the period during which the asset is used.

Factors in Computing Depreciation

There are several methods of computing depreciation. Whichever method is used, the following factors must be taken into consideration for each asset:

Cost of the asset.
Its estimated useful life.
Estimated salvage or trade-in value at the end of its useful life.

The Straight-Line Method of Depreciation

The simplest and most commonly used method of computing depreciation is known as the *straight-line method.* Under this method, the estimated salvage value and any additional first-year depreciation taken [1] are subtracted from the cost. The remainder is divided by the estimated useful life of the asset. The resulting figure is the amount to be charged off as depreciation each accounting period.

---

[1] Regardless of which method you use for computing depreciation, Federal income-tax regulations allow you, under certain conditions, to take an additional 20 percent "first-year depreciation." For more information about this possibility, consult the IRS publication *Tax Information on Depreciation.*

For example, assume that a piece of equipment is bought for $1,000. Its salvage value is estimated at $60, and its useful life at 10 years. If the straight-line method of depreciation is used, the annual depreciation will be computed as follows:

$$\frac{\$1,000 - \$60}{10} = \$94.$$

If the depreciation is to be charged off each month, the amount entered will be $\frac{1}{12}$ of $94, or $7.83.

Other Depreciation Methods

The *sum-of-the-years-digits method* and the *double-declining-balance method* (described below) are based on the idea that an asset depreciates faster during the early years of its life than in the later years. The *total* depreciation that can be charged off is the same as under the straight-line method, but some of it can be charged off sooner. This provides a tax reduction in the earlier years. Other things being equal, a corresponding tax increase will occur in later years, but you will have had the use of the money for several years.

The amount that can be charged off in any one accounting period is limited to twice the depreciation available under the straight-line method in the case of new assets purchased. For used assets purchased, the limit is 1½ times the straight-line amount. Also, these methods can be used only for depreciating assets whose useful lives are estimated to be 3 years or more.

You may choose which method of depreciation to use for each asset you purchase. For tax purposes, however, the same method must be used over the life of the asset unless you get permission from the Commissioner of Internal Revenue to change the method. There is one exception to this rule: You may change from the double-declining-balance method to the straight-line method without this special permission.

Sum-of-the-Years-Digits Method

In the sum-of-the-years-digits method, the depreciation rate of an asset for any year is a fraction whose numerator is the remaining years of life of the asset (at the beginning of the year) and whose denominator is the sum of the numerators. For an asset with a 4-year life, for example, the sum-of-the-years-digits method would give the following depreciation rates:

Year	Remaining life at beginning of year	Rate for the year
1...................	4	4/10 or 40 percent
2...................	3	3/10 or 30 percent
3...................	2	2/10 or 20 percent
4...................	1	1/10 or 10 percent
Total.........	10	10/10 or 100 percent

As in the straight-line method, these rates are applied to the cost minus the salvage value and minus any additional first-year depreciation taken. Also, if the asset purchased is used equipment, the first year's depreciation may not be more than $1\frac{1}{2}$ times what it would be under the straight-line method. In the above example, the straight-line depreciation for 1 year would be 25 percent. Therefore, for an asset purchased secondhand, the first year's depreciation using the sum-of-the-years-digits method could be only 37.5 percent instead of the 40 percent shown in the example. The remaining 3 years would have to absorb the 2.5 percent difference.

Double-Declining-Balance Method

Under the double-declining-balance method, the depreciation rate for each year is double the straight-line rate ($1\frac{1}{2}$ times for used assets purchased). This higher rate, however, is applied only to the amount of the asset cost that has not yet been charged off. A new asset that cost $10,000 and had an estimated useful life of 4 years would be depreciated at a rate of 50 percent per year (twice the straight-line 25 percent) applied as follows:

Year	Undepreciated basis at beginning of year	Depreciation at 50 percent of remaining balance
1....................	$10,000	$5,000
2....................	5,000	2,500
3....................	2,500	1,250
4....................	1,250	625

Undepreciated at end of asset's useful life, $625.

Under this method, the complete cost of the asset will never be charged off as depreciation. The undepreciated amount at the end of the useful life of the asset is considered salvage value. The original basis of $10,000 is therefore the full cost of the asset; no deduction is made for salvage value. An adjustment for additional first-year depreciation might be made, however.

Amortizing Leasehold Improvements

Leasehold improvements are improvements to leased property that become the property of the owner when the lease ends.· If these improvements are made in place of rent, their cost may be deducted as rent. If they are made in addition to rent, they are recorded as property costs by the tenant. In the latter case, if the useful life of the improvements is less than the remaining life of the lease, they are depreciated, or *amortized*, like other assets. However, if the useful life of the improvements is longer than the remaining life of the lease, the straight-line method must be used and the remaining life of the lease is used in the computation instead of the estimated useful life of the improvement.

Recording the Purchase and Depreciation of Plant Assets

Generally, a separate account is set up in the *General Ledger* for each major class of property, such as furniture and fixtures, delivery equipment, buildings, leasehold improvements, and so on. Sometimes, however, more than one depreciation rate or method is applied to different items in one class of equipment. When that happens, separate accounts should be set up for the property to which each rate or method is applied. These separate accounts may be either in the *General Ledger* or in subsidiary accounts that are summarized in a *General Ledger* account.

Recording the Purchase

If equipment is purchased for cash or on an account to be paid in a short time, the entry is made in the *Cash Disbursements, Purchases, and Expense Journal* at the time payment is made. The amount will be entered in the Amount-of-Check column and in the General Ledger debit column with the account shown as the name of the asset purchased.

Often equipment is purchased with a down payment and a note for the balance payable over a number of months or years. In this case, the down payment is entered in the Amount-of-Check column; the unpaid balance as a credit under General Ledger Items, with the account shown as "Notes payable"; and the total cost as a debit under General Ledger Items with the name of the asset purchased shown as the account. Interest should not be included in the cost of the equipment; it should be treated as an expense when it is paid.

As payments are made on the note, the amount of the payment is entered (1) in the Amount-of-Check column, and (2) as a debit in the General Ledger column with the account shown as "Notes payable." If part of the payment applies to interest, this amount is entered as a debit under Miscellaneous Income and Expense Items, and the remainder is debited to Notes Payable in the General Ledger column.

An example. Suppose you purchase a counter for $700. You make a down payment of $100 and sign a note for the balance at 6 percent per year, to be paid at the rate of $100 a month. The entries in the *Cash Disbursements Journal* for the purchase and the first payment on the note will be as follows:

Transaction	Description or account	Column	Amount
Purchase	Furniture and fixtures	General ledger items (dr.) Amount of check (cr.)	$700 100
	Notes payable	General ledger items (cr.)	600
First payment	Notes payable	Amount of check (cr.) General ledger items (dr.)	$103 100
	Interest	Miscellaneous income and expense items (dr.)	3

Purchase of a going business. If you buy a going business for a lump sum, the amount paid may not be the same as the value of the business shown on the books of the former owner. This creates the problem of distributing the purchase price among the various assets purchased. To avoid income-tax problems, you should consult an accountant or other qualified tax practitioner before recording the transaction in your books.

Depreciation Schedules

Depreciation can be computed separately for each item of property in your business. It is simpler, however, and usually just as satisfactory

Exhibit 17.—Depreciation Schedule: Delivery Trucks—Straight Line—5 years

Date		Cost	Allowance for Depreciation	1970	1971	1972	1973	1974	1975	1976	Remaining Balance
1970	(Salvage value $500)	4500 00	400 00	400 00							(Salv) 500 00
	Balance 12-31-70	4500 00	400 00		800 00				400 00		
1971	Balance 12-31-71	4500 00	1200 00			800 00					
			800 00								
1972	Balance 12-31-72	4500 00	2000 00				800 00	800 00			
1973	(Salvage value $500)	5400 00	1290 00				490 00	980 00	980 00	980 00	1470 00
	Balance 12-31-73	9900 00	3290 00				1290 00				(Salv) 500 00
7-1-74	Disposal of 1970 truck	⟨4500 00⟩	⟨3200 00⟩					⟨400 00⟩	⟨400 00⟩	980 00	⟨500 00⟩
			1380 00					1380 00		1470 00	
1974	Balance 12-31-74	5400 00	1470 00								

to group all items of a given class (equipment, machinery, buildings, and so on) for which the same method of depreciation is used and estimate an average rate of depreciation for each group.

A *depreciation schedule* should be set up for each group of assets and each method of depreciation used. Exhibit 17 is an example of a depreciation schedule for delivery trucks that are depreciated on a straight-line basis.

The first two dollar columns of this schedule show the cost of the assets and the accumulated allowance for depreciation. Each of the other columns except the last one provides for scheduling 1 year's depreciation. The last column is used for the salvage value and the balance that will remain after the last year for which there is room on the schedule. This balance and the salvage value are carried forward to the next sheet.

At the end of each year, equipment or other depreciable property purchased during the year is recorded on the proper depreciation schedule. The probable depreciation will have to be computed in the meantime for your monthly statements; but you may not want to make some decisions final (what method of depreciation to use, whether to take additional first-year depreciation, and so on) until you know what the year's profit picture is going to be. Any difference between the estimated and actual depreciation for the year can be adjusted when the final month's entry is made.

To record the purchase of equipment on the depreciation schedule, enter the salvage value in the Description column and the cost in the Cost column. Then compute the annual depreciation for that purchase and distribute it, with the salvage value, in the years' and Remaining-Balance columns.

Whether or not any equipment has been purchased during the year, at the end of each year all depreciation for that year is transferred, or closed, into the Accumulated-Allowance column. At all times, the Accumulated-Allowance column *plus* all "open" years' depreciation *plus* the total of the Remaining-Balance column should equal the total of the Cost column.

Thus, in exhibit 17, at the end of 1974 the figures should be checked in the following manner:

$$1470+(400+980-400)+980+(500+1470+500-500)=5400.$$

The totals of the Cost and Accumulated-Allowance columns should equal the balances of the corresponding accounts in the *General Ledger* as of the end of the year.

Theoretically, depreciation of each addition to the Cost column for the year of purchase should be computed on the basis of the remaining months of the year. You will find it much simpler, however, to use an average of 6 months' depreciation. Income-tax regulations do not specifically provide for this method, but the Internal Revenue Service allows it if it is used consistently and does not result in a gross overstatement of depreciation in any one year.

An example. In exhibit 17, it is assumed that the business opened in 1970. A truck was purchased at that time for $4,500 and another one 3 years later—in 1973—for $5,400. Thus, the 12–31–73 Cost and Accumulated-Depreciation balances include both trucks. Then, since the older truck is disposed of in 1974, the 12–31–74 balances include only the truck purchased in 1973.

In each case, the salvage value was estimated at $500 and the useful life of the equipment at 5 years. Depreciation is computed by the straight-line method. For the truck purchased in 1970, this means that $4,000 is to be depreciated at an annual rate of ⅕ of $4,000 or $800. Allowing 6 months' depreciation, or $400, for the first year leaves $400 to be depreciated in 1975.

The truck purchased in 1973 is depreciated at the rate of $980 a year. Again, 6 months' depreciation is charged in the first and last years. The salvage value will remain on the schedule until the truck is disposed of.

Recording the Depreciation in Your Books

Although depreciation is computed on an annual basis, you need to know each month's depreciation for use in preparing monthly financial statements. For assets on hand at the beginning of the year, the monthly depreciation can be computed from the depreciation schedules simply by dividing the total depreciation scheduled for that year by 12. When additional property is purchased during the year, the year's depreciation on it should be estimated and from this figure, the depreciation for the month. The total monthly depreciation is then increased by this amount.

For example, in exhibit 17, at the beginning of 1973, you know there will be a year's depreciation of $800.00 on the truck then on hand. You will therefore have monthly depreciation on this truck of $800÷12, or $66.67. In *March 1973,* you buy the second truck. At that time, you estimate that you will have depreciation in 1973 of $490.00 on the new truck. This amount will be recorded ⅒, or $49.00, in each of the months from March to December. Your total depreciation for each of these months will therefore be $66.67+$49.00, or $115.67. Total depreciation for the year 1973 will thus agree with exhibit 17:

2 months (January and February) at $66.67 _____ $ 133. 34
10 months (March through November at $115.67;
    December $115.63 to adjust for fractions) _____ 1, 156. 66

Total for the year _____ $1, 290. 00

As explained earlier, the new truck will not be entered on the depreciation schedule until the end of the year. It is possible that you may decide then to use a different method of computing depreciation from the one you used in recording the estimated monthly depreciation. If that happens, you should adjust the final month's depreciation entry in your books so that the year's total will be equal to the depreciation shown for that year on the schedule.

The monthly depreciation is entered in your *Cash Disbursements, Purchases, and Expense Journal*—as a debit in the Miscellaneous-Income-and-Expense-Items column, with the account shown as "Depreciation," and as a credit in the General-Ledger column, with the account shown as "Allowance for depreciation of *(name of asset account)*."

In recording property and depreciation, it is important that your books be kept strictly in accordance with Federal income-tax requirements. If you are doing business in a State whose requirements differ from the Federal requirements, you may have to keep separate property records for State-tax purposes.

The Internal Revenue Service publishes a useful guide to the handling of depreciation from the standpoint of Federal income-tax regulations—*Tax Information on Depreciation.* See page 135 for further information.

Recording the Sale, Trade-in, or Junking of Plant Assets

The salvage value of a fully depreciated asset remains on the depreciation schedule, and the cost and accumulated allowance for depreciation remain in the *General Ledger* accounts, until the asset is disposed of. Disposal of an asset will be one of the following:

Sale of a fully depreciated asset.
Sale of an asset that still has book value. (The *book value* of an asset is its undepreciated balance, or the original cost less the accumulated depreciation.)
Trade-in of a fully depreciated asset.
Trade-in of an asset that still has book value.
Junking of a fully depreciated asset.
Junking of an asset that still has book value.

The entries necessary for each of these types of disposal are explained below and tabulated in exhibit 18.

Exhibit 18.—Entries for Recording Disposal of Plant Assets in the Journals.

	Transaction	Amount to be entered	Account shown as:	Column in which amount is entered
Enter in Cash Receipts Journal	Sale of fully depreciated asset	Amount of cash received	Gain or loss on disposal of assets	Total cash deposit, and Miscellaneous income and expense (*credit*)
		Cost of the asset	(*Name of asset account*)	General ledger (*credit*)
		Cost of the asset	Allowance for depreciation of (*name of asset account*)	General ledger (*debit*)
	Sale of asset with book value	Cost of the asset	(*Name of asset account*)	General ledger (*credit*)
		Difference between cash received and book value	Gain or loss on disposal of assets	Miscellaneous income and expense (*credit* if cash received is more than book value; *debit* if less)
		Amount of cash received		Total cash deposit
		Accumulated allowance for depreciation	Allowance for depreciation of (*name of asset account*)	General ledger (*debit*)
Enter in Cash Disbursements Journal	Trade-in of fully depreciated asset	Cash paid for new asset	(*Name of payee*)	Amount of check
		Difference between cash paid and cost of old asset	(*Name of asset account*)	General ledger (*debit* if cash paid is more than cost of old asset; *credit* if less)
		Cost of old asset	Allowance for depreciation of (*name of asset account*)	General ledger (*debit*)
	Trade-in of asset with book value	Cash paid for new asset	(*Name of payee*)	Amount of check
		Difference between cost of new asset (cash paid + book value of old asset) and original cost of old asset	(*Name of asset account*)	General ledger (*debit* if cost of new asset is more than cost of old asset; *credit* if less)
		Accumulated allowance for depreciation	Allowance for depreciation of (*name of asset account*)	General ledger (*debit*)
	Junking of fully depreciated asset	Cost of the asset	Allowance for depreciation of (*name of asset account*)	General ledger (*debit*)
		Cost of the asset	(*Name of asset account*)	General ledger (*credit*)
	Junking of asset with book value	Book value of the asset	Loss on abandonment of property	Miscellaneous income and expense (*debit*)
		Cost of the asset	(*Name of asset account*)	General ledger (*credit*)
		Accumulated allowance for depreciation	Allowance for depreciation of (*name of asset account*)	General ledger (*debit*)

Sale of a Fully Depreciated Asset

When a fully depreciated asset is sold, whatever amount you receive is a gain and should be recorded as such. This is done by entering the amount received from the *Daily Summary* (miscellaneous receipts) to the Total-Cash-Deposit column of the *Sales and Cash Receipts Journal* and to the credit column under Miscellaneous Income and Expense Items with the account shown as "Gain or loss on disposal of assets."

Entries must also be made to remove the cost of the asset and the allowance for depreciation from the *General Ledger*. This is done by making two offsetting entries for the amount of the asset's cost in the General-Ledger columns of the journal. A credit entry is made with the account shown as the proper asset account—for example, "Furniture and fixtures." The other entry is a debit with the account shown as "Allowance for depreciation of furniture and fixtures" (or whatever type of asset has been sold).

Sale of an Asset With Book Value

The sale of an asset that has an undepreciated balance on the books can result in either a gain or a loss. It depends upon whether you sell it for more or less than the undepreciated balance. If there is a gain, the following entries are made in the *Sales and Cash Receipts Journal:*

Enter the amount received from the *Daily Summary* to the Total-Cash-Deposit column.

Enter the gain (cash received less book value) in the Miscellaneous-Income-and-Expense-Items *credit* column, with the account shown as "Gain or loss on disposal of assets."

Enter the cost of the asset in the General-Ledger-Items credit column with the asset account shown.

Enter the accumulated allowance for depreciation in the General-Ledger debit column with the account shown as "Allowance for depreciation of (*name of asset account*)."

If the sale results in a loss, the entries are the same except for the second one, which will be as follows:

Enter the loss (book value less cash received) in the Miscellaneous-Income-and-Expense-Items *debit* column with the account shown as "Gain or loss on disposal of assets."

Trade-in of an Asset

The Internal Revenue Service does not recognize any gain or loss from the trade-in of an asset. If the asset traded in still has book value, this book value is considered as part of the cost of the new asset. Thus, the cost basis of the new asset becomes the cash actually paid for it *plus* the book value of the asset traded. No recognition is given to any trade-in allowance agreed upon by you and the vendor.

Trade-in of an asset with book value. Assume that an adding machine is purchased for $350.00 with a $50.00 allowance for trade-in of an old adding machine. This leaves a net cash payment of $300.00. The old adding machine was purchased for $250.00, and allowance for its depreciation totaled $212.50 by the date of the trade-in, leaving a book value of $37.50. The new machine will thus have a cost basis of $337.50 ($300.00 cash plus the $37.50 book value of the old machine).

Since there is already $250.00 in the asset account, another $87.50 must be added to bring it up to the $337.50 cost of the new machine. Also, since there is no depreciation on the new machine as yet, the $212.50 depreciation on the old machine must be removed from the Allowance-for-Depreciation account. The entry in the *Cash Disbursements, Purchases, and Expense Journal* is therefore as follows:

$300.00 in the Amount-of-Check column.

$87.50 in the General-Ledger debit column with the account shown as "Furniture and fixtures."

$212.50 in the General-Ledger debit column with the account shown as "Allowance for depreciation—furniture and fixtures."

Trade-in of a fully depreciated asset. If the machine traded in had been fully depreciated and therefore had no book value, the cost basis for the new machine would be simply the $300.00 cash paid. The entries would be as follows:

$300.00 in the Amount-of-Check column.

$50.00 in the General-Ledger debit column with the account shown as "Furniture and fixtures."

$250.00 in the General-Ledger debit column with the account shown as "Allowance for depreciation—furniture and fixtures."

Junking of an Asset

The junking of an asset is recorded through the *Cash Disbursements, Purchases, and Expense Journal*. This is done for convenience' sake even though no cash is involved.

If the asset to be junked is *fully depreciated*, two entries are made under General Ledger Items. In both entries, the amount to be entered is the original cost of the asset. One entry is made in the debit column with the account shown as "Allowance for depreciation—(*name of asset account*)." The other entry is made in the credit column with the asset account shown.

If the asset is junked when it *still has a book value*, three entries are needed:

> The book value is entered in the debit column under Miscellaneous Income and Expense Items with the account shown as "Loss on abandonment of property."
>
> The cost of the asset is entered in the credit column under General Ledger Items with the asset account shown.
>
> The accumulated allowance for depreciation is entered in the debit column under General Ledger Items with the account shown as "Allowance for depreciation—(*name of asset account*)."

Any loss on abandonment of property should be kept in a separate account from losses on sale of property. Under some circumstances, the two types of losses are treated differently for tax purposes.

Recording Disposal of Property on the Depreciation Schedule

Disposal of an asset must be recorded on the depreciation schedule as well as in the journals. The entries on the schedule remove the cost basis of the property from the Cost column, the depreciation allowed to the date of the disposal from the Allowance-for-Depreciation column, and any remaining depreciation from "open" depreciation columns. Gain or loss on the disposal will not affect nor appear on the depreciation schedule.

Referring to exhibit 17, suppose that the delivery truck purchased in 1970 had been disposed of on July 1, 1974. At that time, depreciation of this truck accounted for $3,200 of the Allowance-for-Depreciation balance—$400 in 1970, $800 each year for the next 3 years, and $400 for 6 months of 1974. Therefore, the following entries, *all deductions,* will be made on the depreciation schedule (see "7–1–74" entry on exhibit 17):

> $4,500 in the Cost column.
> $3,200 in the Depreciation Allowance column.
> $400 in the 1974 column, to eliminate the last half year's depreciation.
> $400 in the 1975 column.
> $500 in the remaining-balance column.

These entries will be the same regardless of whether the truck was sold, traded in, or junked and regardless of whether or not it was disposed of at a profit. If the truck is traded in, the new truck will be entered on the depreciation schedule with the cost recorded as the book value of the old truck (in the above example $1,300) plus the cash paid.

All entries of disposals on the depreciation schedules should show the date of disposal and the year in which the property was purchased.

Part 10

Here They Come—Taxes!

Collecting and Recording Sales Taxes............... 115

    Methods of Handling Sales Taxes........................ 115

    Recording Payment of Sales Taxes 119

Payroll Records and Payroll Taxes.................. 119

    Payroll Records.. 123

    Payroll Taxes.. 123

Income and Self-Employment Taxes................. 126

    Types of Federal Income-Tax Returns.................... 126

    Investment Credit 130

    Self-Employment Taxes................................. 130

    Declaration of Estimated Taxes......................... 130

    Information Returns.................................... 132

    State Income Taxes.................................... 132

    Recording Income Taxes............................... 132

Collecting and Recording Sales Taxes

A majority of the 50 States and many cities or other local jurisdictions have sales taxes. In some cases, both State and local taxes are assessed. It is usually the duty of the retailer to collect these taxes.

A number of factors complicate the collection and recording of sales taxes. Few, if any, States have one flat sales-tax rate for all sales. There may be more than one tax rate, depending on the type of items sold, and some items may be entirely exempt from the sales tax.

There are also exemptions based on the status of the purchaser. These might include sales to governmental agencies, certain public institutions, foreign diplomats, and persons who will resell the goods. Often individual sales of very small amounts are tax exempt.

The element of "breakage" also complicates the recording and reporting of sales-tax collections. Computing a sales tax exactly by applying the tax rate to the amount of the sale would often give fractions of cents. Because of this, most taxing jurisdictions specify sales-amount brackets to which certain amounts of taxes apply. Fractions of cents are usually rounded to the next higher cent in these tables, so that a little more than the tax rate is collected. Where the retailer is allowed to compute the amount he owes by applying the tax rate to his total taxable sales, a certain amount of breakage will accrue to the benefit of the retailer.

Methods of Handling Sales Taxes

The first requirement of the system you use for collecting, recording, and reporting sales taxes is that the system must meet the requirements of the taxing jurisdiction in which your business is located. Get in touch with the taxing authorities in your area for sales-tax regulations. If there is any doubt in your mind as to whether the system you want to use meets the requirements, describe it to the taxing authorities and ask them for suggestions.

115

Several different systems of recording sales-tax collections are described here. Which one is best suited to your needs will depend on the nature of your business and the sales-tax regulations in your area.

Method I. You can use this method of recording sales taxes if (1) all your sales are subject to sales tax, *and* (2) a separate accounting for sales-tax collections is not required by law. When you ring up a sale on the cash register or prepare a sales check, compute the sales tax and record it as a part of the total sales. This means that the sales figures entered on the *Daily Summary* will include the sales tax.

After the month's transactions have been entered in the journal, compute the total sales tax for the month as follows:

1. Add the Total-Sales column. This will give a preliminary total that includes the sales tax.
2. Divide this preliminary total by 1 plus the sales-tax rate to get the sales-only figure.
3. Multiply the sales-only figure by the sales-tax rate to get the sales tax.

You can check your computation by adding the sales tax to the sales-only figure. This should give the original column total.

For example, suppose the Total-Sales column adds up to $6,221.64. With a sales-tax rate of 3 percent, the sales tax is computed as follows:

$$\text{Sales only} = \$6,221.64 \div 1.03 = \$6,040.43.$$
$$\text{Sales tax} = \$6,040.43 \times .03 = \$181.21.$$
$$\text{Check: } \$6,040.43 + \$181.21 = \$6,221.64.$$

To enter the sales tax in the *Sales and Cash Receipts Journal*, write "Sales tax" in the description column and enter the sales-tax amount (1) in the Total-Sales column, circled or in red to show a deduction, and (2) in the credit column under General Ledger Items. The General-Ledger item will be posted to a liability account headed "Sales Tax Payable."

Method II. If almost all of your sales are subject to sales tax but an occasional tax-exempt sale occurs, Method I can still be used with a little modification. A record is kept of all tax-exempt sales, both charge and cash. At the end of the month, these sales are totaled and subtracted from the total of the Total Sales column in the *Cash Receipts Journal*. The resulting figure will include only *taxable* sales and sales tax and is used instead of the column total in computing the amount of the sales tax.

Method III. If a substantial number of your sales are subject to sales tax, but also a substantial number are not, you may have to record taxable sales and sales-tax collections separately. If you use sales checks, this is simply a matter of totaling tax-exempt sales, taxable sales, and sales-tax collections separately. If you use a cash register, you can have it equipped with taxable-sales and sales-tax keys. Each taxable item is rung up on the taxable-sales key. If a sale includes more than one taxable item, a subtotal of all these items is obtained and the tax computed for this subtotal. The sales tax is then rung up on the sales-tax key.

If you use this method, the *Daily Summary of Sales and Cash Receipts* should be revised to provide a separate record of taxable sales and sales tax, as shown in exhibit 19. Separate columns should also be provided in the *Sales and Cash Receipts Journal* for total taxable sales and total sales tax (see exhibit 20, p. 120).

The Taxable-Sales column in the journal will be a memo column only to accumulate the amount to show on your sales-tax report. It is not used in preparing your monthly statements nor posted to the *General Ledger*. The Sales-Tax column will be posted to the *General Ledger* account "Sales Tax Payable."

Method IV. If only a small percentage of your sales are subject to sales tax, you may find it satisfactory just to keep a list of the individual taxable sales (cash and charge) and the taxes on them. The taxes shown on this list can be totaled at the end of the month and entered in the *Sales and Cash Receipts Journal,* as in method I.

Method V. This is the simplest method of handling sales-tax collections. It consists merely of putting all sales-tax collections in a separate container kept in or near the cash register or till. No record is made of the tax collections until the end of the month, when all the money that has been accumulated in the separate container should be deposited. The amount is recorded in the Cash Receipts section of the *Daily Summary* as "Sales Tax" and entered in the *Cash Receipts Journal* in the credit column under General Ledger Items. This credit will later be posted to the Sales-Tax-Payable account in the *General Ledger*.

Variations of this method are used by a number of small businessmen, but it is not recommended for the following reasons:

• There is usually little control over the amounts of sales-tax collections. Shortages could easily be undetected.

• Change making is more difficult because the cashier must remember to deposit the correct amount in the separate container. As a result, shortages or overages are more likely to occur.

• There is a temptation for the cashier to assume that shortages or overages found in balancing the day's cash are due to errors in handling the sales-tax money and to transfer cash without further checking. Actual recording errors could go undetected.

• If many tax-exempt sales are made, the sales tax collected will be less than the tax rate applied to total sales. In case of an audit by the

Exhibit 19.—Daily Summary Showing Taxable Sales and Sales Tax

DAILY SUMMARY OF SALES AND CASH RECEIPTS

Date March 23, 19—

CASH RECEIPTS

1. Cash sales	$429. 00	
1b. Sales tax on cash sales	6. 00	$435. 00
2. Collections on account		100. 00
3. Miscellaneous receipts [1]		15. 00
4. TOTAL RECEIPTS TO BE ACCOUNTED FOR.		$550. 00

CASH ON HAND

5. Cash in register or till:		
Coins	$ 25. 00	
Bills	510. 00	
Checks	95. 00	
Total cash in register or till		$630. 00
6. Petty-cash slips		14. 00
7. TOTAL CASH ACCOUNTED FOR		$644. 00
8. Less change and petty-cash fund:		
Petty-cash slips	$14. 00	
Coins and bills	86. 00	
Change and petty-cash fund (fixed amount)..		100. 00
9. TOTAL CASH DEPOSIT		$544. 00
10. CASH SHORT (Item 4 less item 9 if item 4 is larger).		$ 6. 00
11. CASH OVER (Item 9 less item 4 if item 9 is larger).		$ ——

TOTAL SALES

	Taxable sales (memo only)	Sales tax	Total sales (ex- cluding sales tax)
	(a)	(b)	(c)
12. Cash sales	$200. 00	$6. 00	$429. 00
13. Charge sales (sales checks #262 to #316)	100. 00	3. 00	222. 00
14. TOTAL SALES	$300. 00	$9. 00	$651. 00
15. TOTAL CHARGES TO CUSTOMERS (13b+13c).			$225. 00

By John Doe

[1] Note to appear on back of summary: "Miscellaneous receipts: Refund on merchandise $15.00."

taxing authorities, you could have trouble proving that this difference was due to exempt sales.

- This method cannot be used unless *all* sales are for cash.

Other methods. Several other methods or variations of the above methods could be used. For example, if your business is departmentalized, one department may sell almost entirely nontaxable items and another, almost entirely taxable items. It may be possible to arrange the departments so that one or more of them sells entirely nontaxable items. No record of sales taxes would then have to be kept in these departments.

Recording Payment of Sales Taxes

When and how you pay sales taxes will depend on the regulations of the taxing authority in your area. Be sure that you understand what is required of you.

When you make the payment, it will be entered in the *Cash Disbursements Journal.* The account is shown as "Sales Tax" and the amount is entered in the Amount-of-Check column and in the debit column under General Ledger Items. The debit entry will later be posted to the Sales-Tax-Payable account in the *General Ledger.*

Payroll Records and Payroll Taxes

If you have any employees at all, you have certain obligations to the Federal Government for payment of payroll taxes and withholding of income taxes in connection with the salaries of your employees. You will probably have similar obligations for payroll and/or withholding taxes to the State and perhaps to the local jurisdiction—it depends on where your business is located. Contact city and State authorities for information about payroll and withholding taxes under their jurisdictions.

Exhibit 20.—Sales and Cash Receipts Journal Showing Taxable Sales and Sales Tax

Date	Description and/or Account	PR	Total Sales (CR)	Taxable Sales (Memo)	Charges to Customers (DR)	Collections on Account (CR)	Sales Tax (CR)	Miscellaneous Income and Expense Items (DR)	Miscellaneous Income and Expense Items (CR)	General Ledger Items (DR)	General Ledger Items (CR)	Total Cash Deposit (DR)
19__												
May 23	Daily Summary		651 00	300 00	225 00	100 00	9 00					544 00
	Refund on merchandise								15 00			
	Cash short							6 00				

Federal regulations do not prescribe the form in which your payroll records must be kept, but the records should include the following information and documents:

1. The name, address, and Social Security number of each employee.

2. The amount and date of each wage payment and the period covered by the payment.

3. The amount of wages subject to withholding included in each payment.

4. The amount of withholding tax collected and the date it was collected.

5. If applicable, the reason that the taxable amount is less than the total payment.

6. Your employer identification number.

7. Duplicate copies of returns filed.

8. Dates and amounts of deposits made with Govenment depositories.

9. The periods for which your employees are paid by you while they are absent because of sickness or personal injury, and the amount and weekly rates of the payments.

10. Your employees' withholding exemption certificates.

11. Any agreement between you and an employee for withholding of additional amount of tax.

You will also have to keep these documents and records.

1. Copies of statements furnished by employees relating to nonresident alien status, residence in Puerto Rico or Virgin Islands, or residence or physical presence in a foreign country.

2. The value and date of any noncash compensation paid to a retail salesperson from which no tax was withheld.

3. The dates in each calendar quarter on which an employee performed services not in the course of your trade or business, and the amount you paid for these services.

4. Copies of employees' statements of tips they received in the course of their employment, unless this information is reported on another item in this list.

5. Employees' requests to have their withholding tax computed on the basis of their cumulative wages.

Regarding Social Security (FICA) taxes, you must maintain these additional records.

1. The amount of wages that are subject to FICA tax.

Exhibit 21

EMPLOYEE COMPENSATION RECORD

NAME _____ SOC. SEC. NO. _____

ADDRESS _____ DATE OF BIRTH _____

PHONE _____ RATE _____ NO. OF EXEMPTIONS _____

Pay period ending	Hours worked							Total regular hours	Over-time	Earnings			Deductions						Net pay
	S	M	T	W	Th	F	S			At regular rate	At overtime rate	Total	Social security	Fed. income tax	State income tax	Group insurance	U.S. bonds	Other	
QUARTERLY TOTALS																			

2. The amount and date of FICA employee tax collected for each payment and the date collected.

3. If applicable, the reason that the total wage payment and the taxable amount are not equal.

Under the Federal Unemployment Tax Act, you must maintain these records.

1. The total amount you paid your employees during the calendar year.

2. The amount of the wages subject to the unemployment tax, and, if applicable, why this amount differs from the total compensation.

3. The amount you paid into the State unemployment fund, showing the payments deducted or to be deducted, and the payments not deducted or to be deducted from your employees' wages.

Payroll Records

Usually, an employee's earnings card is set up for each employee. Every wage payment to the employee is recorded on this card—all the information needed for meeting Federal and State or city requirements relating to payroll and withholding taxes, and all other amounts deducted from the employee's wages.

A number of payroll-records systems are available commercially. Most of these are based on the pegboard or multiple-copy principle. A single writing of a check or payslip to be given to the employee makes a carbon entry on the employee's earnings card and on a payroll summary or journal for each pay period. If you have only one or two employees, however, it should not be necessary to have a special payroll system. Paychecks can be entered directly in your *Cash Disbursements Journal* as described in part 3 and on an earnings card for each employee. Earnings cards are available from most stationers who handle office supplies. A typical one is shown as exhibit 21.

If you do not want to enter the individual employees' wages in the *Cash Disbursements Journal,* they can be entered on the earnings cards only. The gross salaries, each type of deduction, and net salaries can then be totaled and the totals entered in the journal.

Payroll Taxes

There are three types of Federal payroll taxes: (1) income taxes withheld, (2) Social Security taxes, and (3) Federal Unemployment taxes.

Income taxes are withheld on all wages paid an employee above a certain minimum. This minimum is governed by the number of withholding allowances claimed by the employee.

Social Security taxes apply to only the first $15,300 (as of January 1, 1976) of wages paid an employee during a year. A percentage deduction from the employee's wages is matched by a tax paid by the employer.

Federal unemployment taxes are required only of employers "who during the current or preceding calendar year paid wages of $1,500 or more in any calendar quarter, or at any time had ONE or more employees for some portion of at least 1 day during each of 20 different calendar weeks." This tax is paid by the employer (no deduction is made from the employee's wages) on the first $4,200 of wages paid the employee. You may receive a credit against your Federal unemployment taxes for a certain percentage of the State unemployment taxes you pay. Instructions accompanying the *Employer's Annual Federal Unemployment Tax Return* (form 940) explain the filing requirements and tax computation more fully.

The rates as well as the bases for each of these taxes change from time to time as new legislation is passed. The *Employer's Tax Guide* (*circular E*), published by the Internal Revenue Service, gives detailed instructions about these obligations.

As an employer, you are in effect an agent for the Government in collecting income, Social Security, and Federal unemployment taxes. As these taxes accumulate, you must deposit them in a bank that is authorized to collect them—either a Federal Reserve Bank or an authorized commercial bank. The next section describes the guidelines you must follow in making these required deposits.

Payment of payroll taxes. If your total liability is less than $200 per quarter—that is, if the income tax plus employer and employee social security taxes total less than $200 for the designated 3 month period—no deposit is necessary. The total amount of the taxes you owe may be submitted with the quarterly return that is due on or before the last day of the month following the close of the quarter.

If at the end of the first month in the quarter, your tax liability is less than $200, but by the end of the second month, the cumulative liability is $200 or more, then you must deposit the cumulative amount by the 15th day of the 3d month of the quarter. The liability for the third month may then be submitted with the quarterly return on or before the last day of the month following the close of the quarter.

If the cumulative liability does not reach $200 until the third month, the total liability must be deposited by the last day of the month following the close of the quarter.

If your cumulative liability is more than $200 but less than $2,000 for each of the first 2 months in the quarter, deposits must be made on or before the 15th day of the next month. For the last month, the deposit must be made on the last day of the month following the close of the quarter.

Other deposit rules are applicable if your undeposited Social Security taxes (employer and employee) plus income taxes withheld from your employees amount to $2,000 or more at the end of any monthly period. These requirements are given in detail in *Employers Tax Guide* (circular E). (See For Further Information.)

To make deposits, a form 501, *Federal Tax Deposit, Withheld Income and FICA Taxes,* should be filled in and submitted with the deposit to an authorized commercial bank or Federal Reserve Bank.

Although your return for Federal unemployment taxes is only filed once a year (on or before January 31 of the following year), you must make a deposit of taxes if your liability exceeds $100 for any calendar quarter and any preceding quarter. Your deposit must be made with an authorized bank within 1 month following the close of the quarter. Once a deposit is made you must start accumulating the taxable wages paid (only those under $4,200 for the year) to determine whether additional deposits are required. If deposits of unemployment taxes have been made, you report these with your annual return and pay any balance due.

Recording payroll taxes. Your bookkeeping can ·be simplified to some extent if, at the end of each month, you draw the required check to the depository and enter it for that month in the *Cash Disbursements Journal.* The entries are as follows:

Amount entered	*Column*
Total amount of check.	Amount of Check.
Amount representing income taxes withheld.	Payroll Deductions—Income tax (*as a deduction*).
Amount representing Social Security tax deducted from employees' wages.	Payroll Deductions—Social Security (*as a deduction*).
Amount representing your share of the Social Security tax.	Miscellaneous Income and Expense Items (*debit column*).

The total of the last three items should equal the amount of the check. If this is done every month, the deductions in the two payroll-deduction columns will exactly offset all other entries in these columns. The columns will total zero and so will not have to be posted to the *General Ledger.*

State income taxes withheld are handled in much the same way, except that payments will probably be required only at the end of the quarter. State unemployment taxes are usually paid quarterly also.

Both Federal and State unemployment taxes are an expense to you as the employer. They are entered in the *Cash Disbursements Journal*, with the description "payroll taxes." The amounts of the payments should be entered in the amount-of-check column and also in the debit column under miscellaneous income and expense items.

Income and
Self-Employment Taxes

The discussion of Federal income taxes presented here does not go into technical instructions for preparing your tax returns. These instructions are best obtained from the *Tax Guide for Small Business* issued each year by the Internal Revenue Service. See page 135 for further information about the *Guide*.

Requirements for preparing and filing Federal income-tax returns are more complicated for a business than for an individual. In deciding whether to prepare your own tax returns or hire someone to do it, you should consider the complexity of your business and whether you or one of your employees has the necessary skills. Usually, a more accurate return can be prepared by someone who is thoroughly familiar with Federal income-tax regulations. Many attorneys specialize in income-tax work, and nearly all practicing certified public accountants and public accountants prepare many tax returns each year.

Types of Federal Income-Tax Returns

The type of Federal income-tax return you file will generally be governed by the form of your business organization. If your business is operated as an *individual proprietorship*—that is, if you are the sole owner and the business is not incorporated—you will report your business operations on Schedule C, to be attached to the Form 1040 you file as an individual.

If your business is a *partnership*, the business must file a Form 1065. No Federal income tax has to be paid by the partnership as such, but the individual partners will report their shares of the profit or loss of the partnership on the Form 1040 which they file as individuals.

If your business is a *corporation*, the corporation must file a Form 1120 and pay a tax on the taxable income reported. Any salaries or dividends paid by the corporation to you must be reported on the Form 1040 you file as an individual.

Corporation tax returns are due on the 15th day of the third month following the close of the taxable year; individual and partnership returns, a month later.

Under certain conditions, the Internal Revenue Code allows an unincorporated business to be taxed as a corporation, and the income of a corporation to be taxed to its individual stockholders. Study these pro-

Exhibit 22

SCHEDULE C (Form 1040) Department of the Treasury Internal Revenue Service	**Profit or (Loss) From Business or Profession** (Sole Proprietorship) Partnerships, Joint Ventures, etc., Must File Form 1065. ► Attach to Form 1040. ► See Instructions for Schedule C (Form 1040).	**1975**

Name(s) as shown on Form 1040	Social security number

A Principal business activity (see Schedule C Instructions) ►..; product ►..

B Business name ►..   C Employer Identification number ►.................................

D Business address (number and street) ►...

City, State and ZIP code ►...   **C**

E Indicate method of accounting: (1) ☐ Cash (2) ☐ Accrual (3) ☐ Other ►..

	Yes	No
F Were you required to file Form W–3 or Form 1096 for 1975? (see Schedule C Instructions)		
If "Yes," where filed ►...........		

G Was an Employer's Quarterly Federal Tax Return, Form 941, filed for this business for any quarter in 1975? . . . .

H Method of inventory valuation ►.. Was there any substantial change in the manner of determining quantities, costs, or valuations between the opening and closing inventories? (If "Yes," attach explanation) . .

Income

1 Gross receipts or sales $........................ Less: returns and allowances $...................... Balance ►	1	
2 Less: Cost of goods sold and/or operations (Schedule C–1, line 8)	2	
3 Gross profit	3	
4 Other income (attach schedule)	4	
5 Total income (add lines 3 and 4)	5	

Deductions

6 Depreciation (explain in Schedule C–3)	6	
7 Taxes on business and business property (explain in Schedule C–2)	7	
8 Rent on business property	8	
9 Repairs (explain in Schedule C–2)	9	
10 Salaries and wages not included on line 3, Schedule C–1 (exclude any paid to yourself) .	10	
11 Insurance	11	
12 Legal and professional fees	12	
13 Commissions	13	
14 Amortization (attach statement)	14	
15 (a) Pension and profit-sharing plans (see Schedule C Instructions)	15(a)	
(b) Employee benefit programs (see Schedule C Instructions)	(b)	
16 Interest on business indebtedness	16	
17 Bad debts arising from sales or services	17	
18 Depletion	18	
19 Other business expenses (specify):		
(a)		
(b)		
(c)		
(d)		
(e)		
(f)		
(g)		
(h)		
(i)		
(j)		
(k) Total other business expenses (add lines 19(a) through 19(j))	19(k)	
20 Total deductions (add lines 6 through 19(k))	20	

21 Net profit or (loss) (subtract line 20 from line 5). Enter here and on Form 1040, line 28. **ALSO** enter on Schedule SE, line 5(a) . . . . | 21 |

SCHEDULE C–1.—Cost of Goods Sold and/or Operations (See Schedule C Instructions for Line 2)

1 Inventory at beginning of year (if different from last year's closing inventory, attach explanation) . . .	1	
2 Purchases $........................ Less: cost of items withdrawn for personal use $...................... Balance ►	2	
3 Cost of labor (do not include salary paid to yourself)	3	
4 Materials and supplies	4	
5 Other costs (attach schedule)	5	
6 Total of lines 1 through 5	6	
7 Less: Inventory at end of year	7	
8 Cost of goods sold and/or operations. Enter here and on line 2 above	8	

visions carefully if you think they could bring tax savings to your business. It would be wise, too, before making your decision, to consult an accountant or attorney who is thoroughly familiar with the technicalities of these provisions.

The first pages of Schedule C (Form 1040), Form 1065, and Form 1120 are shown as exhibits 22, 23, and 24. You will see that similar

Exhibit 23

Form **1065** Department of the Treasury Internal Revenue Service	**U.S. Partnership Return of Income** FOR CALENDAR YEAR 1975 or other taxable year beginning ...., 1975, and ending .... 19......	**1975**
A Principal business activity (See page 7 of instructions)	Name	D Employer identification no.
B Principal product or service (See page 7 of instructions)	Number and street	E Business code no. (See page 7 of instructions)
C Enter total assets from line 13, column (D), Schedule L $	City or town, State, and ZIP code	F Date business commenced

IMPORTANT—Fill in all applicable lines and schedules. If the lines on the schedules are not sufficient, see Instruction P. Enter any items specially allocated to the partners on Schedule K, line 15, instead of the numbered lines on this page or in Schedules D through J. (See General Instruction O.)

	INCOME		
	1a Gross receipts or sales $ .... 1b Less returns and allowances $ .... Balance ▶	1c	
	2 Less: Cost of goods sold and/or operations (line 34, Schedule A)	2	
	3 Gross profit	3	
	4 Ordinary income (loss) from other partnerships, syndicates, etc. (attach statement)	4	
	5 Nonqualifying dividends (attach list—see Instruction 5)	5	
	6 Interest	6	
	7 Rents (Schedule H)	7	
	8 Royalties (attach schedule)	8	
	9 Net farm profit (loss) (attach Schedule F (Form 1040))	9	
	10 Net ordinary gain (loss) (Form 4797, line 9)	10	
	11 Other income (attach schedule)	11	
	12 TOTAL income (lines 3 through 11)	12	

	DEDUCTIONS		
	13 Salaries and wages (other than to partners)	13	
	14 Payments to partners—Salaries and interest	14	
	15 Rent	15	
	16 Interest (attach schedule)	16	
	17 Taxes (attach schedule)	17	
	18 Bad debts (Schedule I if you use reserve method)	18	
	19 Repairs	19	
	20 Depreciation (Schedule J)	20	
	21 Amortization (attach schedule)	21	
	22 Depletion (attach schedule)	22	
	23a Retirement plans, etc. (other than amounts for partners—see Instruction 23a). (Enter number of plans ▶...........)	23a	
	23b Employee benefit programs (see Instruction 23b)	23b	
	24 Other deductions (attach schedule)	24	
	25 TOTAL deductions (lines 13 through 24)	25	
	26 Ordinary income (loss) (line 12 less line 25) (see General Instruction G)	26	

Schedule A—COST OF GOODS SOLD AND/OR OPERATIONS (See Instruction 2)

27 Inventory at beginning of year (if different from last year's closing inventory, attach explanation)		27	
28a Purchases $ .... 28b Less cost of items withdrawn for personal use $ .... Balance ▶		28c	
29 Cost of labor		29	
30 Material and supplies		30	
31 Other costs (attach schedule)		31	
32 Total of lines 27 through 31		32	
33 Less: Inventory at end of year		33	
34 Cost of goods sold. Enter here and on line 2, above		34	

Inventory valuation method ▶

Was there any substantial change in the way you determined quantities, costs or valuations between the opening and closing inventories? . . . . ☐ Yes ☐ No
If "Yes," attach explanation.

Under penalties of perjury, I declare that I have examined this return, including accompanying schedules and statements, and to the best of my knowledge and belief it is true, correct, and complete. If prepared by a person other than partner or member, the preparer's declaration is based on all information of which the preparer has any knowledge.

▶ ....
Signature of partner or member   Date

▶ ....
Signature of preparer other than partner or member   Preparer's address   Date

information is required for all these forms and that the information corresponds to the information included in your statement of profit and loss (exhibit 7). The same general forms have been in use for a number of years with only minor changes.

In addition to the pages shown, a number of supporting schedules are usually required. The information for these schedules will be readily available from your records if you have followed the suggestions made in this booklet.

Exhibit 24

| Form **1120** Department of the Treasury Internal Revenue Service | **U.S. Corporation Income Tax Return** For calendar year 1975 or other taxable year beginning _____, 1975, ending _____ 19___ (PLEASE TYPE OR PRINT) | **1975** |

Check if a—	Name	D Employer identification number
A Consolidated return ☐		
B Personal Holding Co. ☐	Number and street	E Date incorporated
C Business Code No. (See page 7 of instructions)	City or town, State, and ZIP code	F Enter total assets from line 14, column (D), Schedule L (See instruction R) $

IMPORTANT—Fill in all applicable lines and schedules. If the lines on the schedules are not sufficient, see instruction N.

GROSS INCOME	1 Gross receipts or gross sales.................Less: Returns and allowances...............	1	
	2 **Less:** Cost of goods sold (Schedule A) and/or operations (attach schedule)	2	
	3 Gross profit	3	
	4 Dividends (Schedule C)	4	
	5 Interest on obligations of the United States and U.S. Instrumentalities	5	
	6 Other interest	6	
	7 Gross rents	7	
	8 Gross royalties	8	
	9 (a) Net capital gains (attach separate Schedule D)	9(a)	
	(b) Ordinary gain or (loss) from Part II, Form 4797 (attach Form 4797)	9(b)	
	10 Other income (see instructions—attach schedule)	10	
	11 TOTAL income—Add lines 3 through 10	11	
DEDUCTIONS	12 Compensation of officers (Schedule E)	12	
	13 Salaries and wages (not deducted elsewhere)	13	
	14 Repairs (see instructions)	14	
	15 Bad debts (Schedule F if reserve method is used)	15	
	16 Rents	16	
	17 Taxes (attach schedule)	17	
	18 Interest	18	
	19 Contributions (not over 5% of line 30 adjusted per instructions—attach schedule)	19	
	20 Amortization (attach schedule)	20	
	21 Depreciation (Schedule G)	21	
	22 Depletion	22	
	23 Advertising	23	
	24 Pension, profit-sharing, etc. plans (see instructions) (enter number of plans ▶ _____) . .	24	
	25 Employee benefit programs (see instructions)	25	
	26 Other deductions (attach schedule)	26	
	27 TOTAL deductions—Add lines 12 through 26	27	
	28 Taxable income before net operating loss deduction and special deductions (line 11 less line 27)	28	
	29 **Less:** (a) Net operating loss deduction (see instructions—attach schedule) . . 29(a)		
	(b) Special deductions (Schedule I) . . . . 29(b)		
	30 Taxable income (line 28 less line 29)	30	
TAX	31 TOTAL TAX (Schedule J)	31	
	32 Credits: (a) Overpayment from 1974 allowed as a credit . .		
	(b) 1975 estimated tax payments		
	(c) Less refund of 1975 estimated tax applied for on Form 4466 . ( )		
	(d) Tax deposited with Form 7004 (attach copy)		
	(e) Tax deposited with Form 7005 (attach copy)		
	(f) Credit from regulated investment companies (attach Form 2439)		
	(g) U.S. tax on special fuels, nonhighway gas and lubricating oil (attach Form 4136) . .		
	33 TAX DUE (line 31 less line 32). See instruction G for depositary method of payment	33	
	34 OVERPAYMENT (line 32 less line 31)	34	
	35 Enter amount of line 34 you want: Credited to 1976 estimated tax ▶ _____ Refunded ▶	35	

Under penalties of perjury, I declare that I have examined this return, including accompanying schedules and statements, and to the best of my knowledge and belief it is true, correct, and complete. Declaration of preparer (other than taxpayer) is based on all information of which the preparer has any knowledge.

| The Internal Revenue Service does not require a seal on this form, but if one is used, please place it here. | Date _____ | Signature of officer | Title |
| | Date _____ | Signature of individual or firm preparing the return | Preparer's address |

Investment credit

You are allowed an "investment credit" which is deductible directly from your Federal income tax for most depreciable, tangible property. You are allowed this investment credit if the property is used as an integral part of manufacturing, production, extraction, etc., and if you purchased the property in connection with your business or for the production of income. This credit is generally not applicable to buildings or their structural components. The rates of this credit vary with the lives of the property and may change from time to time or be eliminated entirely by changes in the tax law. In some cases you may be entitled to an investment credit on property you lease if the lessor is willing to let you take the credit rather than taking it himself.

Exhibit 25 shows the form provided for the computation of the investment credit (form 3468). This same form is used whether your business is operated as an individual proprietorship, a partnership, or a corporation. Instructions accompanying this form give much more detail on the computation and applicability of this credit than is given here. If you think you are eligible for an investment credit, you should obtain a copy of this form and study the instructions.

Self-Employment Taxes

If you are the owner of an individual proprietorship or if you are a partner in a partnership, the amounts you withdraw from the business are not reportable for the Federal payroll taxes discussed in the preceding section of this booklet. However, unless you had wages from another source subject to the maximum amount reportable for Social Security taxes, you will have to pay, in place of Social Security taxes, a *self-employment tax* based on your income from the business. Although the self-employment tax is not an income tax, the computation is done on Schedule SE (Form 1040) and filed with your individual Federal income-tax return.

Declaration of Estimated Taxes

If you are self-employed, you may be required to file a declaration of estimated tax, even though a wage earner with the same income would not have to do so. This is because income taxes are not withheld from your self-employment income as they are in the case of a wage earner. Current regulations require that you file a declaration and make quarterly payments on the estimated tax if your estimated tax liability is $100 or more and if your estimated income not subject to withholding is more than $500. If you are a wage earner in addition to being self-employed, or if your wife or husband is a wage earner and you plan to file a joint return, wages as well as business income should be included in your estimate.

If your business is a partnership, each of the partners will have to make estimates if they are required to do so as individuals.

If your business is a corporation, it does not have to file a formal declaration of estimated tax. But if the estimated tax is expected to be $40 or more, it must be paid in quarterly installments. The *Tax Guide for Small Business* gives the requirements for computing and making these payments.

Exhibit 25

Form **3468**	**Computation of Investment Credit**	**1975**
Department of the Treasury Internal Revenue Service	▶ Attach to your tax return	

Name	Identifying number as shown on page 1 of your tax return

Note: *Include your share of investment in property made by a partnership, estate, trust, small business corporation, or lessor.*

1 Qualified investment in property acquired or constructed prior to January 22, 1975 and placed in service during the taxable year. (See instructions C and D for eligible property.)

Type of property		Line	(1) Life years	(2) Cost or basis (See instruction G)	(3) Applicable percentage	(4) Qualified investment (Column 2 x column 3)
New property		(a)	3 or more but less than 5		33⅓	
		(b)	5 or more but less than 7		66⅔	
		(c)	7 or more		100	
Used property (See instructions for dollar limitation)		(d)	3 or more but less than 5		33⅓	
		(e)	5 or more but less than 7		66⅔	
		(f)	7 or more		100	

2 Add lines 1(a) through (f) . . . .

3 7% of line 2 (4% for public utility property) . . . .

4 Qualified investment in property acquired or constructed after January 21, 1975 and placed in service during the taxable year, and qualified progress expenditures made after January 21, 1975.

New property		(a)	3 or more but less than 5		33⅓	
		(b)	5 or more but less than 7		66⅔	
		(c)	7 or more		100	
Qualified progress expenditures	1974	(d)	7 or more		20	
	1975	(e)	7 or more		20	
Used property (See instructions for dollar limitation)		(f)	3 or more but less than 5		33⅓	
		(g)	5 or more but less than 7		66⅔	
		(h)	7 or more		100	

5 Add lines 4(a) through (h) . . . .

6 10% of line 5 . . . .

7 Electing corporations with qualifying employee stock ownership plan—Enter 1% of line 5. (Attach election statement.) . .

8 Carryback and carryover of unused credit(s). (See instruction F and instruction for line 8—attach computation.) . . . .

9 Tentative investment credit—Add lines 3, 6, 7, and 8 . . . .

Limitation

10 (a) Individuals—Enter amount from line 16(c), page 1, Form 1040 . . . .⎫

(b) Estates and trusts—Enter amount from line 24 or 25, page 1, Form 1041 . . . . . .⎬

(c) Corporations—Enter amount from line 9, Schedule J, page 3, Form 1120 . . . . . .⎭

11 Less:

(a) Foreign tax credit . . . .

(b) Retirement income credit (individuals only) . . . .

(c) Tax on lump-sum distributions. (See instruction for line 11.) . . . .

12 Total—Add lines 11(a), (b), and (c) . . . .

13 Line 10 less line 12 . . . .

14 (a) Enter amount on line 13 or $25,000, whichever is lesser. (Married persons filing separately, controlled corporate groups, estates, and trusts, see instruction for line 14.) . . . .

(b) If line 13 exceeds line 14(a), enter 50% of the excess. (For public utility property see section 46(a)(6).) . . . . .

15 Total—Add lines 14(a) and (b) . . . .

16 Investment credit—Amount from line 9 or line 15, whichever is lesser (enter here and on line 49, Form 1040; line 10(b), Schedule J, page 3, Form 1120; or the appropriate line on other returns) . . . . . .

Schedule A.—If any part of your investment in lines 1 or 4 above was made by a partnership, estate, trust, small business corporation, or lessor, complete the following statement and identify property qualifying for the 7% or 10% investment credit and qualified progress expenditures.

Name (Partnership, estate, trust, etc.)	Address	Property		
		New	Used	Life years
		$	$	

If property is disposed of prior to the life years used in computing the investment credit, see instruction E.

☼ U.S. GOVERNMENT PRINTING OFFICE 1975 O-575-362 04-2501142

Information Returns

Under certain conditions, your business may be required to file information returns about payments you have made during the year. This information is for use by the Government to verify tax statements made by those receiving the payments. The requirements for filing these returns are explained in the *Tax Guide for Small Business*.

State Income Taxes

Most States and some local jurisdictions have an income tax applicable to businesses. In some cases, the tax returns are very much like those used for Federal taxes. In other areas, an entirely different approach is used. Many States also require information returns.

Contact the local tax authorities in your area and find out what requirements apply to your business. If these requirements differ from those for Federal income-tax returns, make sure that your recordkeeping system will give you the necessary information.

Recording Income Taxes

If your business is an individual proprietorship or a partnership, or if it is a corporation but elects to pay Federal income taxes as a partnership or individual, you ordinarily will not record these taxes on your business books. However, if the business pays taxes as a corporation, the taxes should be entered as an expense of the business. They should be recorded each month so that your monthly statements of profit and loss will not be misleading.

The exact amount of the tax, of course, cannot be computed until the end of the year, so the monthly tax entries will have to be estimated. This can be done as follows:

1. Estimate your total profit for the year and the tax on this profit.
2. Divide the estimated tax by the estimated profit.
3. Multiply the month's profit by the answer obtained in Step 2.

In estimating the income tax for the year, be sure to take into account any losses carried over from previous years. These could reduce or eliminate entirely the tax being estimated. Also, your business might show a loss for 1 or more months during the year. If that happens, no income-tax is entered for those months. Instead, a deduction may have to be entered to reduce the income taxes entered for previous months to the point where the year-to-date tax is the correct percentage of the year-to-date profit. State income taxes are handled in the same manner.

The sum of the estimated State and Federal income taxes for the month (if both are applicable) is entered on line 25 of the monthly statement of profit and loss (exhibit 7). It is also entered in the *Cash Disbursements Journal*—in the debit column under Miscellaneous Income and Expense Items, described as "Income taxes," and in the credit column under General Ledger Items described as "Income taxes payable." If the month's operations resulted in a loss instead of a profit and the income tax set up in earlier months had to be reduced, the entry under Miscellaneous Income and Expense Items is in the credit column and the one under General Ledger Items in the debit column.

For Further Information

If you are interested in further study of basic double-entry bookkeeping, your local public library will be able to provide you with accounting textbooks. There are many good ones.

The three publications already mentioned in parts 9 and 10 of the text are essential. They are:

Tax Information on Depreciation—Publication 534

Tax Guide for Small Business—Publication 334

Employer's Tax Guide (Circular E)

These publications are available free from local offices of the Internal Revenue Service or from U.S. Treasury Department, Internal Revenue Service, Washington, D.C. 20224.

Fundamentals of Finance
for the Small Business

Jack Zwick, Ph. D.

CONTENTS

Chapter 1. What is Financial Management_____ 1

Chapter 2. Financial Statements_____ 5

Chapter 3. Ratio Analysis of Financial Statements_____ 18

Chapter 4. Looking Ahead_____ 31

Chapter 5. The Different Types of Financing_____ 41

Chapter 6. Unsecured Borrowings for Working Capital___ 43

Chapter 7. Secured Working Capital Financing_____ 47

Chapter 8. Secured Growth Capital Financing_____ 49

Chapter 9. The Small Business Administration_____ 51

Chapter 10. SBIC's and Other Sources of Venture Capital___ 57

Chapter 11. For Further Information_____ 60

Chapter 1

WHAT IS FINANCIAL MANAGEMENT?

IT TAKES MONEY TO MAKE MONEY. This maxim is a simple way of saying that a business must have financial resources if it is to operate profitably. If you are in retailing or wholesaling, you must keep a stock of goods on hand to sell. You need to extend credit to customers. A bank balance must be maintained for expenses such as paying suppliers and meeting payrolls. Unless you rent your place of business, funds are necessary for investments in land and buildings. If you are a manufacturer, funds are also required for equipment and machinery, for raw materials and supplies, for stocks of goods in the process of manufacture, for finished goods ready for sale.

But having money does not guarantee making money—that is, making a profit. You not only have to have money; you have to use it well. That is why financial management is important.

Financial management includes the following functions:

● Seeing that the assets of the business are used in such a way as to bring the highest possible return on the money invested.

● Evaluating the need for new assets.

● Obtaining funds to finance asset additions.

● Managing both old and new assets so that each contributes its full share toward the profitable operation of the business.

● Repaying borrowed funds from profits those funds have generated.

1

Getting the Financial Resources You Need

Your most important task as financial manager is to find *sources* of funds to offset the company's *uses* of funds. When a need for funds arise:

● You can increase liabilities and/or equity to match the increases in assets.

● Or you can reduce the investment in some existing asset so as to hold down the total investment in assets.

Let's assume, for example, that your business, in order to keep or expand its sales volume, needs to extend more credit to customers for longer periods of time. In other words, the investment in receivables (an asset) must be increased. You may or may not be able to increase your borrowings. That will depend, perhaps, on whether you can convince your banker that the move is a wise one and that the company's financial position is strong enough to warrant a loan. And you may or may not be able to get more equity capital to finance the receivables increase. You might decide, therefore—or be forced—to squeeze down other assets, such as bank balances or inventories, to provide the needed funds. Your job as financial manager is to decide which of these sources can and— even more important in many instances—which one should be tapped for the financial resources you need.

Making a Profit—Your Basic Obligation

A primary reason for owning and operating your own business is to make the highest possible profit for yourself. You also have responsibilities to employees, to customers, to members of the community whose lives your company influences—and these responsibilities are important. But it is you who have taken the risk of contributing capital. Your basic goal is to take care of this capital and use it as profitably as possible.

It is important, therefore, for you to have at your command a useful measure of business performance that emphasizes financial returns. There are several methods of measuring profitability, but one in particular— "return on investment"—is especially useful. Chapter 3 explains how to use this and other profitability measures.

Managing Assets

One of your most important duties as financial manager is to keep the assets of the business working hard and productively. It is easy for a small business to slip into the practice of having larger inventories, bank balances, and other investments than are really needed. "Bigger" is often equated with "better." The sales manager wants larger inventories, more lines of finished stocks, more liberal credit terms. These added investments will improve his sales efforts. The production manager wants newer and faster machines and tools, larger stocks of raw materials and supplies. These investments enable him to cut his costs and meet delivery dates. The financial manager wants larger cash balances to make his job easier. Office management needs new equipment. Often it seems that the opportunties to spend money are unlimited!

The aim of asset management is to make certain that new or increased assets pay their way. The added profits these new assets bring in should total more than the cost of the resources involved. The return-on-investment measure mentioned above can be used to show the expected effect on profits of an investment you may be thinking about making. Thus, it is a useful tool in judging and comparing various investment opportunties.

Often, unfortunately, opportunities that promise satisfactory returns on investment must be put aside because of lack of capital. This is especially true in small businesses, where financing new investments can be a real problem. When such a problem arises, good asset management may come to the rescue in two ways. First, it may improve a small company's chances of getting a loan by emphasizing to the lender the financial competence and alertness of the would-be borrower. Second, additional cash can sometimes be raised by reducing unnecessary investments in existing assets. That is, it may be possible to provide funds for one area of the business by avoiding or reducing their use in other areas.

The Tools of Financial Management

If your financial management is to be more than guesswork, you must have tools to work with. At the least, you need accurate, well-organized accounting records, regular financial reports, and some techniques for analyzing the reports. These tools will not give you readymade answers to your financial problems, but they will help in shaping up sound decisions based on facts and tested principles of business management.

Accounting records. Good accounting records are the foundation on which sound financial management is based. The reports with which a financial manager works can be no more accurate nor complete than the records they summarize.

Accounting records may be simple or complex, depending on the size and nature of the business, but they should be well organized and consistent. The small business that does not have such an accounting system

3

would be wise to have a public accountant set one up and explain its use to the person who will be responsible for maintaining it. Today several service firms have developed "time-shared", computer assisted accounting systems which simplify and speedup the process of getting good financial data on a timely basis. Many small businesses find such systems to be both economic and valuable as a planning tool. Your commercial banks can put you in touch with reputable firms in your business area so that the advisability of computerized bookkeeping can be checked out. Both time and money will be saved in the long run if you have a system.

Financial reports. There are a number of financial reports that can be helpful in financial management. The principal ones are the profit-and-loss statement and the balance sheet. These two financial statements are important to you for several reasons.

First, they are the basis for financial analysis; and as such, they are used by bankers and investors in making loan and investment decisions. If you want to enlist the support of these members of the business community, you should be able to provide the statements and to explain or defend items that appear in them.

Second, State and Federal laws pertaining to taxation and financing require reports that be prepared only from financial statements.

Third, you should be able to read and interpret these statements as part of your management program. Only through careful financial analysis can you find and strengthen the weak spots in your financial policies and plan sound and vigorous programs for the future.

Chapter 2 explains the balance sheet and the profit-and-loss statement in more detail.

Techniques for analyzing financial statements. Various percentages and other measures of comparison have been found useful in interpreting financial statements and highlighting relations between their items. These comparative measures help to answer questions such as these:

Could the company pay its bills if business conditions tightened up temporarily? Is the money I have invested in the business bringing me as much profit as it could? If not, where are the problem areas? What percent profit could I promise an investor if he put some money into the business? Are my inventories working hard enough? Does the record show that the business is strong enough and stable enough to qualify for a long-term loan? Such questions are of interest, not just to the businessman himself, but to his banker, his creditors, possible investors, and others.

Some of the most useful of the techniques for analyzing financial statements are explained and illustrated in chapter 3.

4

FINANCIAL STATEMENTS

T HE TWO MOST IMPORTANT FINANCIAL STATEMENTS are the balance sheet and the profit-and-loss statement. The difference between the two is sometimes explained by comparing the balance sheet to a "still picture" and the profit-and-loss statement to a "moving picture." The balance sheet presents a financial picture of the business—its assets, liabilities, and ownership—*on a given date*. It is usually prepared as of the close of the last day of a month and answers the question, "How did we stand financially at that time?" The profit-and-loss statement (also called the income statement) measures costs and expenses against sales revenues over a definite period of time, such as a month or a year, to show the net profit or loss of the business *for the entire period*. Notice that the balance sheets shown in this chapter (exhibits 1, 2, and 3) are dated simply "December 31, 19—," but the profit-and-loss statements (exhibits 4, 5, and 7) are dated *"For the Year Ended* December 31, 19—."

The Balance Sheet

The balance sheet has two main sections. The first section (the left side if the two sections are shown side by side) shows the assets. The second (or right hand) section shows the liabilities (or debts) and the owner's equity, which together represent the claims against the assets. The total assets always equal the combined total of the liabilities and the owner's equity (or capital)—that is why this financial statement is called a balance sheet.

5

Assets. Anything the business owns that has money value is an asset. The assets of a small business commonly include cash, notes receivable, accounts receivable, inventories, land, buildings, machinery, equipment, and other investments. They are usually classified as current assets, fixed assets, or other assets.

● *Current assets* are cash and assets that are expected to be converted into cash during the normal operating cycle of the business (generally, within a year). They include notes receivable, accounts receivable, marketable securities, and inventories, as well as cash. However, if inventories are not to be used up (that is, converted into accounts receivable or cash) within a year, they should be recorded as fixed assets. The same is true of notes receivable and accounts receivable that are not expected to be converted into cash within a year—they should be treated as fixed assets.

The balance sheet of a small manufacturer typically shows three types of inventories. The *materials and supplies inventory* consists of materials to be used in production, together with supplies used in connection with the processing. *Work in process,* as the name implies, consists of goods in the process of manufacture but not yet completed. *Finished goods* are merchandise completed and ready for sale. Finished goods (or merchandise) and supplies are usually the only inventory items shown on the balance sheet by small retailers and wholesalers.

● *Fixed assets* are those acquired for long-term use in the business. They include land, buildings, plant, machinery, equipment, furniture, fixtures, and so on. These assets are typically not for resale, and they are recorded on the balance sheet at their cost to the business, less depreciation.

A fixed asset is treated as a long-term cost, with the cost allocated as depreciation over the working life of the asset. Thus, the value of a fixed asset shown on the balance sheet is not ncessarily the same as the resale value of the asset.

● *"Other"* assets include patents, trade investments, goodwill, and so on. (Goodwill is recorded on the balance sheet only to the extent that it has actually been purchased.)

Assets are also sometimes classified as *tangible* or *intangible.* Literally, tangible means "able to be physically touched." Current and fixed assets are normally tangible; "other" assets, typically intangible.

Liabilities. Liabilities are the claims of creditors against the assets of the business—in other words, debts owed by the business. They do not include owners' claims. Among the more common liabilities are notes payable, accounts payable, accrued liabilities, and allowance for taxes.

Exhibit 1

The MONAR Company [1]

Balance Sheet

December 31, 19___

Assets

Current assets:

Cash	$20,000	
Accounts receivable	40,000	
Inventories	45,000	
Total current assets		$105,000

Fixed assets:

Machinery and equipment	$20,000	
Buildings	28,000	
Land	12,000	
Total fixed assets		60,000

Total assets		$165,000

Liabilities and Equity

Current liabilities:

Accounts payable	$20,000	
Notes payable	30,000	
Accrued liabilities	6,000	
Reserve for taxes	4,000	
Total current liabilities		$60,000

Equity:

Capital stock	$50,000	
Surplus	55,000	
Total equity		105,000

Total liabilities and equity		$165,000

[1] Not a real company.

Exhibit 2

The MONAR Company [1]

Balance Sheet
December 31, 19__

Assets

Current assets:

Cash		$20,000	
Accounts receivable	$40,000		
Less allowance for doubtful accounts	3,000	37,000	
Inventories	$45,000		
Less allowance for inventory loss	5,000	40,000	
Total current assets			$97,000

Fixed assets:

Machinery	$20,000		
Less allowance for depreciation	4,000	$16,000	
Buildings	$28,000		
Less allowance for depreciation	6,000	22,000	
Land		12,000	
Total fixed assets			50,000
Total assets			$147,000

Liabilities and Equity

Current liabilities:

Accounts payable	$20,000	
Notes payable	30,000	
Accrued liabilities	6,000	
Allowance for taxes	4,000	
Total current liabilities		$60,000

Equity:

Capital stock	$50,000	
Surplus	37,000	
Total equity		87,000
Total liabilities and equity		$147,000

[1] Not a real company.

Current liabilities are those due for payment within a year. *Long-term (or fixed) liabilities* are debts, or parts of debts, that are *not* due for payment within a year. The *allowance for future income taxes* represents the taxes that will have to be paid on the profits of the current year, but that are not due for payment until later. *Accrued liabilities* are similar to the allowance for future income taxes in that the expenses are charged against profits of the current year, although payment will not be made until later. The most common example is accrued wages, which must be accounted for whenever the last day of the accounting period does not coincide with the last day of a pay period.

Equity. The assets of a business minus its liabilities equal the equity. This equity is the investment of the owner or owners plus any profits that have been left to accumulate in the business (or minus any losses).

If the business is incorporated, its books will show a capital stock account. This account represents the paid-in value of the shares issued to the owners of the business. Undistributed profits are recorded in an earned-surplus account. If the business is a proprietorship or a partnership, the capital accounts appear under the name or names of the owners. Increases in equity as a result of undistributed earnings are also recorded there, as are decreases in equity if the business shows a loss instead of a profit.

Valuation accounts. Depreciation and other factors reduce the value of some assets. Because it is important to state balance-sheet values correctly, the balance sheet is usually set up in such a way as to show that provision has been made for such reductions in value. This is done by using depreciation, or valuation, accounts. Some of the more common of these accounts are the following:

• *Accounts receivable* are analyzed according to the length of time the money has been owed. An estimate is then made of what proportion of them will turn out to be uncollectable. This "allowance for bad debts" is usually computed for a given accounting period either as a percentage of the average balance of receivables or as a percentage of the net credit sales for the period. The balance sheet shows it as a deduction from the asset "accounts receivable."

• *Losses in the value of inventories* may occur as a result of price changes, style changes, physical deterioration, pilferage, and so on. If such losses are likely to occur, an estimate of possible shrinkage should be made. This estimate appears on the balance sheet as a deduction from the value of the inventory.

9

Exhibit 3

Monroe Manufacturing Company [1]

Balance Sheet
December 31, 19__

Assets

Current assets:

Cash		$40,000
Accounts receivable	$90,000	
Less allowance for doubtful accounts	10,000	80,000
Inventories:		
Finished product	75,000	
Work in process	75,000	
Raw materials	20,000	
Supplies	10,000	180,000
Prepaid expenses		10,000
Total current assets		$310,000
Fixed assets:		
Furniture and fixtures	$10,000	
Less allowance for depreciation	5,000	$5,000
Machinery and equipment	$30,000	
Less allowance for depreciation	16,000	14,000
Buildings	$45,000	
Less allowance for depreciation	9,000	36,000
Land		15,000
Total fixed assets		70,000
Investments		20,000
Total assets		$400,000

Liabilities and Equity

Current liabilities:

Accounts payable		$40,000
Notes payable		80,000
Accrued liabilities:		
Wages and salaries payable	$4,000	
Interest payable	1,000	5,000
Allowance for taxes		
Income tax	$16,000	
State taxes	4,000	20,000
Total current liabilities		$145,000
Equity:		
Capital stock	$200,000	
Surplus	55,000	
Total equity		255,000
Total liabilities and equity		$400,000

[1] Not a real company.

• *Fixed assets,* other than land, decline in value. This decline in value may be due to wear and tear, technical obsolescence, and other causes. A periodic charge for depreciation should be made and shown on the balance sheet as a deduction from the value of the asset.

Some Examples

Exhibit 1 shows a simple balance sheet. It represents the financial position of the Monar Company,[1] a retail enterprise, on December 31, 19—. Total assets of $165,000 are offset by liabilities and equity totaling $165,000. The balance sheet balances. The assets are grouped as current assets and fixed assets (Monar has no "other assets"). Current liabilities are identified as such, although there are no long-term liabilities.

When the valuation accounts are included in the balance sheet, the statement becomes more accurate and therefore more useful. Exhibit 2 shows how they affect the asset figures that appear in exhibit 1. Note the following changes:

1. Accounts receivable have been reduced by $3,000 to an estimated $37,000, all collectible.

2. Inventory values have been reduced by $5,000 to $40,000.

3. Total current assets, therefore, show a reduction of $8,000 from $105,000 to $97,000.

4. Machinery is now valued at $16,000, or $4,000 less than the original $20,000.

5. The value of the buildings has been reduced by $6,000 to $22,000.

6. Total fixed assets have thus declined by $10,000.

7. Total assets have declined by $18,000.

8. Surplus is now $37,000 and total equity $87,000, each one $18,000 less than in exhibit 1.

9. Total liabilities and equity now balance total assets at $147,000.

The balance sheet shown in exhibit 3 has been expanded still further to make it even more useful. This is the relatively detailed statement of a typical small manufacturer.

The Profit-and-Loss Statement—A Retailer or Wholesaler

A profit-and-loss statement of the Monar Company, whose balance sheet appears in exhibits 1 and 2 is shown in simplified form as exhibit 4. A brief explanation of the items is given here:

---

[1] Not a real company.

Sales. The item "sales" includes all sales of merchandise or services. The sales figure shown in exhibit 4 represents net sales. It is computed by subtracting sales discounts and sales returns and allowances from gross sales.

Cost of goods sold. The "cost of goods sold" is the total price paid for the products sold during the accounting period, plus in-transportation costs. Most small retail and wholesale businesses compute cost of goods sold by adding the value of the goods purchased during the accounting period to the beginning inventory, and then subtracting the value of the inventory on hand at the end of the accounting period.

Selling expenses. These are expenses incurred directly or indirectly in making sales. They include salaries of the sale force, commissions, advertising expense, out-freight if goods are sold f.o.b. destination, and so on. Shares of rent, heat, light, power, supplies, and other expenses that contribute to the company's sales activities may also be charged to selling expense. In small businesses, however, such mixed expenses are usually charged to general expenses.

General and administrative expenses. General salaries and wages, supplies, and other operating costs necessary to the overall administration of the business are in this group of expenses.

Nonoperating income. Some small businesses receive additional income from interest, dividends, miscellaneous sales, rents, royalties, gains

Exhibit 4

The MONAR Company [1]
Profit–and–Loss Statement
For the Year Ended December 31, 19—

Sales		$120,000
Cost of goods sold		70,000
Gross margin		$50,000
Selling expenses:		
Salaries	$15,000	
Commission	5,000	
Advertising	5,000	
Total selling expenses		25,000
Selling margin		$25,000
Administrative expenses		10,000
Net profit		$15,000

[1] Not a real company.

---

on sale of capital assets, and so on. In such cases, the "net profit" shown in exhibit 4 is really a net operating profit. The nonoperating income would be added to it and any interest paid subtracted. The result would then be the net profit before State and Federal income taxes.

Exhibit 5 shows, in more detail than is given in exhibit 4, a profit-and-loss statement for a small wholesale business. The retailer's statement of exhibit 4 would appear much the same if shown in similar detail.

Exhibit 5

Wald Wholesale Company [1]

Profit-and-Loss Statement
For the Year Ended December 31, 19__

Net sales			$666,720
Cost of goods sold:			
Beginning inventory, January 1, 19__		$184,350	
Merchandise purchases	$454,920		
Freight and drayage	30,210	485,130	
Cost of goods available for sale		$669,480	
Less ending inventory, December 31, 19__		193,710	
Cost of goods sold			475,770
Gross margin			$190,950
Selling, administrative, and general expenses:			
Salaries and wages		$88,170	
Rent		24,390	
Light, heat, and power		8,840	
Other expenses		21,300	
State and local taxes and licenses		5,130	
Depreciation and amortization on leasehold improvements		4,140	
Repairs		2,110	
Total selling, administrative, and general expenses			154,080
Profit from operations			$36,870
Other income		$7,550	
Other expense		1,740	5,810
Net profit before taxes			$42,680
Provision for income tax			15,120
Net profit after income tax			$27,560

[1] Not a real company.

13

Profit-and-Loss Statement of a Small Manufacturer

Because the small manufacturer converts raw materials into finished goods, his method of accounting for cost of goods sold differs from the method for wholesalers and retailers. As in retailing and wholesaling, computing the cost of goods sold during the accounting period involves beginning and ending inventories, and purchases made during the accounting period. But in manufacturing it involves, not only finished-goods inventories, but also raw-materials inventories, goods-in-process inventories, direct labor, and factory-overhead costs.

To avoid a long and complicated profit-and-loss statement, the cost of goods manufactured is usually reported separately. Exhibits 6 and 7 show a statement of cost of goods manufactured and a profit-and-loss statement for a typical small manufacturing company. A few of the terms used are explained below.

Raw materials are the materials that become a part of the finished product.

Direct labor is labor applied directly to the actual process of converting raw materials into finished products.

Manufacturing overhead includes depreciation, light, insurance, real estate taxes, the wages of foremen and others who do not work directly on the product, and so on—in other words, all manufacturing costs except raw materials and direct labor.

Interpreting the Profit-and-Loss Statement

Notice, in the profit-and-loss statements shown in exhibits 4, 5, and 7, that the *gross margin* (sometimes called gross profit) is computed first, and then the net profit. The gross margin equals sales less cost of sales. It does not take into account the overhead expenses (other than factory overhead) of being in business, the selling expenses, office expenses, and so on. The Hayes Manufacturing Company [1] (exhibit 7) reports a gross margin of $96,000 on net sales of $669,100. The gross-margin percentage, then, is about 14 percent. This indicates that the goods sold cost the company about $86 per $100 of sales.

The net profit of the business is the final profit after all costs and expenses for the accounting period have been deducted. The Hayes Manufacturing Company made a net profit of $25,360, or about 4 percent on net sales.

---

[1] Not a real company.

Exhibit 6

Hayes Manufacturing Company [1]

Statement of Cost of Goods Manufactured
For the Year Ended December 31, 19___

Work-in-process inventory, January 1, 19___			$18,800
Raw materials:			
Inventory, January 1, 19___		$154,300	
Purchases		263,520	
Freight In		9,400	
Cost of materials available for use		$427,220	
Less inventory, December 31, 19___		163,120	
Cost of materials used		$264,100	
Direct labor		150,650	
Manufacturing overhead:			
Indirect labor	$23,750		
Factory heat, light, and power	89,500		
Factory supplies used	22,100		
Insurance and taxes	8,100		
Depreciation of plant and equipment	35,300		
Total manufacturing overhead		178,750	
Total manufacturing costs			593,500
Total work in process during period			$612,300
Less work-in-process inventory, December 31, 19___			42,600
Cost of goods manufactured			$569,700

[1] Not a real company.

15

Exhibit 7

16

Hayes Manufacturing Company [1]

Profit-and-Loss Statement
For the Year Ended December 31, 19___

Net sales			$669,100
Cost of goods sold:			
Finished goods inventory, January 1, 19___		$69,200	
Cost of goods manufactured (exhibit 6)		569,700	
Total cost of goods available for sale		$638,900	
Less finished goods inventory, Dec. 31, 19___		66,400	
Cost of goods sold			572,500
Gross margin			$96,600
Selling and administrative expenses:			
Selling expenses:			
Sales salaries and commissions	$26,700		
Advertising expense	12,900		
Miscellaneous selling expense	2,100		
Total selling expenses		$41,700	
Administrative expenses:			
Salaries	$27,400		
Miscellaneous administrative expense	4,800		
Total administrative expenses		32,200	
Total selling and administrative expenses			73,900
Net operating profit			$22,700
Other revenue			15,300
Net profit before taxes			$38,000
Estimated income tax			12,640
Net profit after income tax			$25,360

[1] Not a real company.

Use With Caution!

The balance sheet tries to present a "true and fair picture" of the financial position of a business *at the close of* the accounting period. The profit-and-loss statement tries to present a "true and fair" picture of the results of operations *during* the accounting period. These reports, constructed according to accepted principles of accounting, are one of the small businessman's most important tools.

But they are drawn up under conditions of uncertainty, and many of the transactions involved are necessarily incomplete at the end of the accounting period. Also, the balance sheets do not reflect resale or liquidating values; they reflect the cost, or cost less depreciation, of the assets held by the business as a going concern. The figures depend to some extent on the judgment of your accountant who has decided which accounting techniques are best suited to your business. These facts should be kept in mind in considering the techniques for analyzing financial statements discussed in the next chapter.

Chapter 3

RATIO ANALYSIS OF FINANCIAL STATEMENTS

THE TWO TYPES OF FINANCIAL STATEMENTS, the balance sheet and the profit-and-loss statement, are necessary—and useful. But they are only a start toward understanding where you stand, where you're going, and how you're going to get there. If you are to get your money's worth out of them (they do take time to prepare), you should study various relations between some of the figures they present.

A number of indicators have been worked out for this purpose. In many ways, these indicators or comparative measures (usually expressed as ratios) are more useful for analyzing your business operations than the dollar amounts. They provide clues for spotting trends in the direction of better or poorer performance. They also make it possible for you to compare your company's performance with the average performance of similar businesses. Some important points must be kept in mind, however.

● *Businesses are not exactly comparable.* There are different ways of computing and recording some of the items on financial statements. As a result, the figures for your business may not correspond exactly to those for the businesses with which you want to compare it.

● *Ratios are computed for specific dates.* Unless the financial statements on which they are based are prepared often, seasonal characteristics of your business may be obscured.

● *Financial statements show what has happened in the past.* An important purpose in using ratios is to obtain clues to the future so that you can prepare for the problems and opportunities that lie ahead. Since the ratios are based on past performance, you must use them in the light of your best knowledge and judgment about the future.

● The ratios are not ends in themselves, but tools that can help answer some of your financial questions. They can do this only if you interpret them with care.

Measure of Liquidity

Liquidity may be thought of simply as ability to pay your bills. It is the first objective of financial management. Measures of liquidity are intended to help you answer questions such as this:

"Do we have enough cash, plus assets that can be readily turned into cash, so that we are sure of being able to pay the debts that will fall due during this accounting period?"

The current ratio. The current ratio is one of the best known measures of financial strength. The main question it answers is this: "Does your business have enough current assets to meet its current debts—with a margin of safety for possible losses such as inventory shrinkage or uncollectable accounts?"

The current ratio is computed from the balance sheet by dividing current assets by current liabilities. For the Ajax Manufacturing Company (exhibit 8), it is computed as follows:

$$\frac{\text{Current assets}}{\text{Current liabilities}} = \frac{\$140,000}{\$60,000} = 2.3 \text{ (or 2.3 to 1)}.$$

Is this a good current ratio? Should the owner of the Ajax Company be reasonably well satisfied with his firm's performance on this point? These questions can't be answered with an unqualified yes or no. A generally popular rule of thumb for the current ratio is 2 to 1, but whether a specific ratio is satisfactory depends on the nature of the business and the characteristics of its current assets and liabilities.

If you decide that your current ratio is too low, you may be able to raise it by:

Paying some debts.
Increasing your current assets from loans or other borrowing with a maturity of *more than a year.*
Converting noncurrent assets into current assets.
Increasing your current assets from new equity contributions.
Plowing back profits.

Exhibit 8

Ajax Manufacturing Company [1]

Combined Balance Sheets

January 1 and December 31, 19___

Assets	December 31, 19___			January 1, 19___		
Current assets:						
Cash		$30,000			$30,000	
Accounts receivable	$42,000			$32,000		
Less allowance for bad debts	2,000	40,000		2,000	30,000	
Merchandise inventory		60,000			50,000	
Prepaid expenses		10,000			10,000	
Total current assets			$140,000			$120,000
Fixed assets:						
Buildings and equipment	$120,000			$120,000		
Less accumulated depreciation	70,000	$50,000		60,000	$60,000	
Land		30,000			30,000	
Total fixed assets			80,000			90,000
Other assets:						
Goodwill and patents			10,000			
Total assets			$230,000			$210,000

Liabilities

Current liabilities:

Accounts payable	$30,000	$25,000
Accrued wages and taxes	10,000	10,000
Estimated income taxes payable	20,000	15,000
Total current liabilities	$60,000	$50,000

Fixed liabilities:

Mortgage bonds, 4 percent	40,000	40,000
Total liabilities	$100,000	$90,000

Equity

Common stock (5,000 shares outstanding)	$60,000	$60,000
Retained earnings	70,000	60,000
Total owner equity	130,000	120,000
Total liabilities and equity	$230,000	$210,000

¹ Not a real company.

21

Let's take some examples. Assume that a small business has the current assets and current liabilities shown in column 1 of exhibit 9. If this firm buys $15,000 worth of merchandise on account (column 2) inventory will be increased to $35,000 and total current assets to $65,000. At the same time, accounts payable will be increased to $35,000 and total current liabilities to $40,000. The current ratio will drop from the present 2.0 to 1.6.

Now going back to the original figures, suppose that the company, instead of buying more merchandise on account, pays bills amounting to $7,000 with cash (column 3). Current assets will then be reduced to $43,000 and current liabilities to $18,000. The current ratio will be increased to 2.4.

Working capital. In neither of the above two instances will there be any change in net working capital (the difference between current assets and current liabilities). But suppose the businessman of exhibit 9, instead of taking either of these steps, invests an additional $10,000 in his business (column 4). This time, current liabilities will not be affected; but current assets will be increased to $60,000, the current ratio will rise to 2.4, and net working capital will be increased from $25,000 to $35,000.

Bankers look at net working capital over periods of time to determine a company's liability to weather financial crises. Loans are often tied to minimum working-capital requirements.

The acid-test ratio. The ratio, sometimes called the "quick ratio," is one of the best measures of liquidity. It is computed as follows:

$$\frac{cash + Government\ securities + receivables}{current\ liabilities}$$

For the Ajax Manufacturing Company, which has no Government securities, this becomes $70,000 divided by $60,000 (see exhibit 8), giving Ajax an acid-test ratio of 1.2 (or 1.2 to 1).

The acid-test ratio is a much more exacting measure than the current ratio. By not including inventories, it concentrates on the really liquid assets, whose values are fairly certain. It helps to answer the question: "If all sales revenues should disappear, could my business meet its current obligations with the readily convertible, 'quick' funds on hand?"

An acid-test ratio of about 1 to 1 is considered satisfactory, subject to the following conditions:

22

Exhibit 9

Effect of Various Transactions on Current Ratio

	(1) Original current assets and current liabilities	(2) Merchandise bought on account ($15,000)	(3) Cash paid on accounts payable ($7,000)	(4) New capital invested ($10,000)
Current assets:				
Cash	$10,000	$10,000	$3,000	$20,000
Accounts receivable	20,000	20,000	20,000	20,000
Inventory	20,000	35,000	20,000	20,000
Total current assets	$50,000	$65,000	$43,000	$60,000
Current liabilities:				
Accounts payable	$20,000	$35,000	$13,000	$20,000
Other	5,000	5,000	5,000	5,000
Total current liabilities	$25,000	$40,000	$18,000	$25,000
Net working capital	$25,000	$25,000	$25,000	$35,000
Current ratio	2.0	1.6	2.4	2.4

• The pattern of accounts receivable collections should not lag much behind the schedule for paying current liabilities. In making this comparison, you should think in terms of paying creditors early enough to take advantage of discounts.

• There should not be much danger of anything happening to slow up the collection of accounts receivable.

Unless you feel comfortable about these two qualifications, you should keep your acid-test ratio somewhat higher than 1 to 1.

A general impression about the current and acid-test ratios is that the higher the ratios the better. This may be true from your creditors' point of view, because they stress prudence and safety. But it is in your interest as owner of the business to be strong and trim, rather than fat. Idle cash balances, and receivables and inventories out of proportion to your selling needs should be reduced. The key to successful financial management is to conserve the resources of your business and to *make these resources work hard for you.* Two measures that are helpful in this connection are average collection period and inventory turnover.

Average collection period. The average collection period, or number of days' sales tied up in accounts receivable, can be computed from the balance sheet and the profit-and-loss statement as follows (the figures used are from exhibits 8 and 10):

Step 1

$$\frac{\text{Net sales}}{\text{days in the accounting period}} = \frac{\$300,000}{365} = \$822, \text{ the average sales per day.}$$

Step 2

$$\frac{\text{Receivables}}{\text{average sales per day}} = \frac{\$40,000}{\$822} = 49, \text{ the number of days' sales tied up in receivables, or average collection period.}$$

Knowing the average collection period helps you answer this question: "How promptly are our accounts being collected, considering the credit terms we extend?" It both suggests the quality of your accounts and notes receivable and tells you how well your credit department is handling the job of collecting these accounts.

The Ajax Manufacturing Company's ratio shows 49 days of sales on the books. To put it another way, accounts are being collected, on the average, in 49 days. A rule of thumb is that the average collection period should not exceed $1\frac{1}{3}$ times the credit terms. If Ajax offers 30 days to pay, therefore, its average collection period should be no more than 40 days. The management should look into the reasons for the slower 49-day period.

The following variations in computing the average collection period are sometimes used for greater accuracy:

- Substitute the total *credit sales* figure for the total sales figure.
- Use an *average receivables* figure. (Add receivables figures for the beginning and the end of the accounting period and divide the result by 2.)
- Compute the average collection period on a *monthly basis*. Trends toward slower collections and serious deviations from your normal collection pattern can then be spotted quickly and remedied. Also, the monthly computation keeps seasonal variations in sales and receivables from distorting the picture. For example, the average collection period of a typical retailer would be overstated if computed on the basis of his annual end-of-the-year balance sheet. At that time of year, his receivables balance is abnormally high because of sales around Christmas.
- In figuring the average sales per day, use the number of *business days* during the accounting period—say, 250 days for the year instead of 365.

Inventory turnover. Inventory turnover shows how fast your merchandise is moving. It gives you an idea of how much capital was tied up in inventory to support the company's operations at the level of the period covered.

Inventory turnover is found by dividing cost of goods sold by average inventory. The Ajax Company, with an inventory of $50,000 at the beginning of the year and an ending inventory of $60,000 (exhibit 8), computes its inventory turnover for the year as follows:

Exhibit 10

Ajax Manufacturing Company [1]

Condensed Profit–and–Loss Statement
For the Year Ended December 31, 19—

Gross sales	$303,000
Less returns and allowances	3,000
Net sales	$300,000
Cost of goods sold	180,000
Gross margin	$120,000
Operating expenses	78,000
Operating profit	$42,000
Interest expense	2,000
Income before taxes	$40,000
Estimated income tax	20,000
Net profit	$20,000

---

[1] Not a real company.

$$\frac{\text{Inventory}}{\text{turnover}} = \frac{\text{Cost of goods sold}}{\text{average inventory}} = \frac{\$180,000}{\frac{1}{2}\ (60,000\ +\ 50,000)} = 3.3$$

This means that Ajax "turned" its inventories 3.3 times during the year—that is, it used up, through operations, merchandise totaling 3.3 times its average inventory investment.

Usually, the higher the turnover, the better. A high turnover means that your company has been able to operate with a relatively small investment in inventory. It may also suggest that your inventories are current and salable; that, since they have not been on the shelves too long, they probably contain few unusable items. But almost anything can be overemphasized, and inventory turnover is no exception. Too much attention to high turnover can lead to inventory shortages and customer dissatisfaction.

What, then, should your inventory turnover be? The desirable rate depends on your line of business, level of business activity, and method of valuing inventories, as well as on various trends. A study of the turnover rates of businesses similar to yours will help you answer the question. Past experience will also serve as a guide.

Exhibit 11

Inventory Turnover by Months, 19___				
	Inventory on 1st of month (1)	Cost of goods sold (2)	Monthly turnover[1] (3)	Annual turnover[2] (4)
January				
February .... 2 months' average......				
March .... 3 months' ave........				
November .... 11 months' average......				
December .... 12 months' average......				

[1] Column 2 divided by column 1.
[2] Column 3 times 12.

Inventory turnover is a much better guide than the absolute size of the inventories. Size can be misleading. An increase in inventories, for instance, may represent the addition of stocks to support growing sales. But it also might mean that merchandise is accumulating because sales have slowed down. In the first case, the inventory turnover remains the same or even increases; in the second case, it declines. Thus, if inventories begin to grow proportionately faster than sales, a declining turnover rate will warn the alert small business owner-manager that trouble is brewing. If inventories are increasing for sound reasons, the turnover will remain the same or improve.

Like the average collection period, inventory turnover should be computed monthly in order to avoid distortions caused by seasonal fluctuations. Records should be cumulative and may take the form shown in exhibit 11.

Inventory turnover records for individual items, groups of products, and product lines are also helpful, especially for retailers and wholesalers. They show which items are selling well and which are slow moving. Such turnovers should be prepared monthly or, for products that are perishable or become obsolete quickly, on a perpetual or daily basis. This enables you to reorder fast-moving items in plenty of time and to prepare to dispose of slow-moving items before their value depreciates too far.

Measures of Profitability

Is your business earning as much profit as it should, considering the amount of money invested in it? This is the second major objective (after liquidity) of financial management, and a number of ratios have been devised to help you measure your company's success in achieving it. A few of them are explained here.

Asset earning power. The ratio of operating profit (earnings before interest and taxes) to total assets is the best guide for appraising the overall earning power of your company's assets. This ratio takes no account of what proportion of the assets represents creditors' equity and what proportion represents your own equity, nor of varying tax rates. For the Ajax Manufacturing Company, it is computed as follows:

$$\frac{\text{Operating profit}}{\text{total assets}} = \frac{\$42,000}{\$230,000} = .18, \text{ or } 18 \text{ percent}$$

Return on the owner's equity. This measure shows the return you received on your own investment in the business. In computing the ratio the average equity is customarily used—the average of the 12 individual months if it is available, or the average of the figures from the beginning and ending balance sheets. For the Ajax Company, the beginning and ending equity figures are $120,000 and $130,000, giving an average of $125,000. The return on the equity is then:

$$\frac{\text{Net profit}}{\text{equity}} = \frac{\$20,000}{\$125,000} = .16, \text{ or } 16 \text{ percent}$$

A similar ratio uses tangible net worth instead of equity. Tangible net worth is the equity less any intangible assets such as patents and goodwill. If there are no intangible assets, there will be no difference between the two values.

Net profit on sales. This ratio measures the difference between what your company takes in and what it spends in the process of doing business. The ratio depends mainly on two factors—operating costs and pricing policies. If your net profit on sales goes down, for instance, it might be because you have lowered prices in the hope of increasing your total sales volume. Or it might be that your costs have been creeping up while prices remained the same.

Net profit on sales is computed as follows:

$$\frac{\text{Net profit}}{\text{Net sales}} = \frac{\$20,000}{\$300,000} = .067, \text{ or } 6.7 \text{ percent.}$$

This means that for every dollar of sales, the company has made a profit of 6.7 cents.

This ratio is most useful when you compare your figures with those of businesses comparable to yours, or when you study the trends in your own business through several accounting periods. Comparing the net profit on sales for individual products or product lines is also useful. Such an analysis will help you decide which products or lines should be pushed.

Investment turnover. Investment turnover is the ratio of annual net sales to total investment. It measures what volume of sales you are getting for each dollar invested in assets. The Ajax Company will compute its investment turnover as follows:

$$\frac{\text{Net sales}}{\text{Total assets}} = \frac{\$300,000}{\$230,000} = 1.3$$

Return on investment (ROI). The rate of return on investment (profit divided by investment) is probably the most useful measure of profitability for the small business owner. Usage varies as to what specific items from the financial statements are to be used for "profit" and "investment." For example, "profit" might be considered to mean net operating profit, net profit before taxes, or net profit after taxes. "Investment" could mean total assets employed or equity alone. It is important to decide which of these values you are going to use in computing return on investment and then to be consistent. In this discussion, *net profit after taxes* and *total assets* will be used. For the Ajax Company, then, the return on investment is computed as follows:

$$\frac{\text{Net profit}}{\text{Total assets}} = \frac{\$20,000}{\$230,000} = .087, \text{ or } 8.7 \text{ percent.}$$

Here's an illustration of the use of the return-on-investment formula: Suppose a small businessman has a total investment of $250,000 in a toy-manufacturing venture and $100,000 in a hotel. He wants to compare the success of these unrelated businesses. The toy manufacturing venture yields annual net profits of $55,000 and the hotel earns $25,000. The return on the toy investment is 22 percent in contrast to 25 percent for the hotel. Other things being equal, the hotel operation is more successful than the toy factory in terms of the return on investment.

Assume, now, that the next year, the businessman wants to increase his toy sales from $500,000 to $600,000 and expects the net income of the toy business to increase from $55,000 to $66,000 as a result. In order to do this, he will have to increase the total investment in the toy concern from $250,000 to $350,000.

The net profit on sales will remain the same—11 percent. The return on investment, however, will drop from 22 percent to 18.8 percent. These changes are shown in the following summary of the toy manufacturing operations:

	Original	Expanded
Investment.........................	$250, 000	$350, 000
Sales..............................	$500, 000	$600, 000
Net profit..........................	$55, 000	$66, 000
Net profit on sales (percent)...........	11.0	11.0
Return on investment (percent)........	22.0	18.8
Investment turnover (times)..........	2.0	1.7

Why did the rate of return on investment drop from 22.0 to 18.8 percent, when the rate of return on sales remained at 11 percent? The answer is found in the investment turnover. A company's net profit on sales may be high; but if the sales volume is low *for the capital invested,* the rate of return on the investment may be low. While the toy manufacturer's profit on sales remained at 11 percent, his investment turnover was only 1.7 the second year compared to 2.0 for the first year. As a result, the return on investment dropped from 22.0 percent to 18.8 percent. On the other hand, the profit on sales can be low and still bring a high return on investment if it is coupled with a high investment turnover.

The toy manufacturing illustration shows why it is important to look at return on investment in addition to sales volume, profit on sales, and absolute profit figures. The investment required to produce the sales and profits are important. The entire triangle of factors—sales, profits, and investment—must be considered in financial management.

Common-Size Financial Statements

Sometimes all values on the financial statements are reduced to percentages. Balance-sheet items are usually expressed as percentages of the total assets figure; profit-and-loss statement items, as percentages of net sales. A statement in this form is often called a "common-size" balance sheet or profit-and-loss statement.

This type of analysis has little or no value, however, unless the percentages are compared with figures for other businesses in the same line of activity or with past records of your own company.

Using the Ratios

Ratios will not provide you with any automatic solutions to your financial problems. They are only tools—though important ones—for measuring the performance of your business. It is the use to which you put them that will determine their real value. Chapter 11 lists a number of sources that publish average ratios for various types of businesses. Compare your ratios with the averages of businesses similar to yours. Also, compare your own ratios for several successive years, watching especially for any unfavorable trends that may be starting.

If warning signs appear, look for the causes and for possible remedies. Studying one ratio in relation to others may help here, but you will probably also need to look into the more detailed records of your business in the areas concerned.

Chapter 4

LOOKING AHEAD

A s your business grows, there will probably be times when you
will need additional funds for investment or operations. You must
be able to plan for these requirements, and to do this you will need
forecasting tools.

The techniques described in this chapter—the cash budget and projected financial statements (sometimes called "pro forma" statements)—
serve many purposes. They help you to keep last-minute decisions and
surprises at a minimum, to set standards of performance for various activities of your business, to anticipate financial needs and the effects of
policy changes. They are a valuable aid in discussions with prospective
lenders. They help you answer such questions as these:

> Will I need additional money?
> When will I need it?
> How long will I need it?
> How much do I need?
> Where can I get it?
> How much will it cost?
> If I borrow it, how can I repay it?

The Cash Budget

The cash budget is simply a plan for cash receipts and expenditures
during a given period. It is one of the most valuable financial tools at
your disposal. By figuring out your cash needs and cash resources ahead
of time, you put yourself in a better position to:

31

Take advantage of money-saving opportunities such as economic order quantities, cash discounts, and so on.
Make the most efficient use of cash.
Finance your seasonal business needs.
Develop a sound borrowing program.
Develop a workable program of debt repayment.
Provide funds for expansion.
Plan for the investment of surplus cash.

How to do it. The length of the period to be covered by the cash budget depends on the nature of your business, how ample your supply of cash is, and how regularly cash flows into and out of your business. The form shown in exhibit 12 (pages 34 and 35) is for a simple cash budget prepared monthly.

The groundwork for preparing a cash budget consists of estimating all cash receipts and cash payments expected during the budget period. Budgets must be carefully planned for cash sales (including discounts and sales returns and allowances), payments of accounts receivable, and any other expected cash income. The same kind of planning must be done for each type of expense that will go to make up the expected cash expenditures. These budgets are based on experience and on the goals you have set for your business.

If expected cash receipts total more than expected cash payments, the difference is added to the expected cash balance at the beginning of the period. If payments total more than receipts, the difference is subtracted. In either case, the result is the expected cash balance at the end of the period.

The cash balance—how much is enough? You must also decide what size cash balance you need to maintain. This, too, is based on experience. You might, for instance, decide that cash equivalent to a certain number of days' sales is a desirable level. If the cash balance at the end of the budgeted period is less than this amount, some short-term borrowing or changes in plans may be necessary. The cash budget, by bringing this to your attention early, gives you time to consider fully all the possible courses of action.

If, on the other hand, the cash balance is larger than you need, the excess can be temporarily invested in marketable securities.

If you need funds—what kind? Cash budgets can help you decide whether you need short-term or long-term capital. A series of 12 monthly cash budgets will show your estimated monthly cash balances for a year. Each of these balances can then be compared with the cash level you have established as desirable for your business. Perhaps your cash balance is ample at the beginning and end of the 12-month period but low at times during the year. This suggests a need for short-term funds. The need will be self-liquidating over the 12-month period.

If, however, cash budgets are developed over longer periods of time and the cash balance is consistently low, the business needs intermediate or long-term capital—intermediate if the need persists for periods lasting from 12 to 30 months, and long-term or permanent capital if it persists for a longer period.

Projected Financial Statements

The cash budget deals with only one account—cash. It is useful to carry your plans for the future a step further by drawing up a profit-and-loss statement and a balance sheet. These statements record your best estimates of what the profitability of your business will be during the period covered and the financial condition of the business at the end of the period. They should be drawn up at least quarterly; and if your business is short of funds, you would be wise to prepare them more often. They will help you avoid unforeseen peak needs that might prove embarrassing.

By providing a look into the future of your business, projected financial statements enable you to judge what the financial needs of your business will be at the end of the forecast period. You can then plan ahead of time whatever steps may be needed to strengthen the business or to prepare for future growth. If you wait until the need actually arises, it will be more difficult and may even be too late.

The projected profit-and-loss statement. The value of the projected profit-and-loss statement as a guide depends largely on your estimate of sales during the period for which the projection is being made. It is therefore well worth your time to develop this estimate as accurately as possible. Use the past experience of the business, figures provided by salesmen, management projections, and any other useful information.

Next, the cost of goods sold must be estimated. A useful first step is to analyze operating data to find out what percentage of sales has gone into cost of goods sold in the past. This percentage can then be adjusted for expected variations in costs, price trends, and efficiency of operations. (A more detailed method estimates each cost item separately and totals the results.)

Other expenses, other income, and taxes can also be estimated on the basis of past experience and expected changes.

Exhibit 12

Cash Budget

For Three Months Ending March 31, 19____

	January		February		March	
	Budget	Actual	Budget	Actual	Budget	Actual
Expected cash receipts:						
1. Cash sales						
2. Collections on accounts receivable						
3. Other income						
4. Total cash receipts						
Expected cash payments:						
5. Raw materials (or merchandise)						
6. Payroll						
7. Other direct factory expenses						

8. Advertising								
9. Selling expense								
10. Administrative expense								
11. Plant and equipment								
12. Other payments (taxes, interest, and so on)								
13. Total cash payments								
14. Expected cash balance at beginning of month								
15. Cash increase or decrease (item 4 minus item 13)								
16. Expected cash balance at end of month (item 14 plus item 15)								
17. Desired cash balance								
18. Short-term loans needed (item 17 minus item 16 if item 17 is larger)								
19. Cash available for short-term investment (item 16 minus item 17 if item 16 is larger)								

A typical projected profit-and-loss statement for the Titan Manufacturing Company is shown in exhibit 13 (page 37).

The projected balance sheet. The projected balance sheet is a summary of the results expected at the end of the period for which the projection is being made. It shows the effect on each balance-sheet item of the sources and uses of funds planned in the various budgets.

The *cash* figure appearing on the projected balance sheet (see exhibit 14 on pages 38 and 39) is the amount decided on as the desirable cash balance in the cash budget. The Titan Company has established 15 days' sales as their desired cash balance. On the basis of the sales estimate of $80,000 for December (exhibit 13), the cash account would be $40,000 on their projected balance sheet.

The *receivables* and *inventory* accounts can be based on past experience and estimated sales. Assume that Titan's receivables have averaged 30 days' sales in the past, and that inventories have been turning roughly one-half times monthly. If other conditions and policies do not change, with Titan's sales estimate of $80,000, receivables should be about $80,000 and inventory $160,000 at the end of the month.

Fixed assets on the estimated balance sheet are based on earlier fixed-asset accounts. That is, the accounts on the most recent balance sheet are adjusted for depreciation and expected additions to or reduction in these assets.

Accrued liabilities and *long-term debts* can usually be assumed to remain unchanged. Of course, if your experience has been that accrued liabilities tend to vary with sales volume, you should take this into account. Any expected increase or reduction in long-term debts during the period should also be given effect.

The *accounts payable* figure is based on an estimate of the number of days' purchases that will be outstanding at the end of the month. Recent and expected purchases and your creditors' terms of sale must be considered.

The *equity* account consists of the existing ownership account plus the earnings to be retained during the period. The amount of retained earnings to be added here comes from the projected income statement. The remaining account, *notes payable* is the last to be computed (unless it has already been determined in connection with the cash budget). Notice that without it, the combined equity and liabilities ($711,000) fall $69,000 short of the total assets ($780,000). This indicates that if the estimates used were reasonably accurate, Titan will need roughly $69,000 of borrowed funds to finance the activities planned.

Exhibit 13

Titan Manufacturing Company [1]

Projected Profit-and-Loss Statement

For the Month Ending December 31, 19___

			Figures based on:
Revenue from sales		$80,000	Sales budget for the month
Cost of sales		56,000	Experience (for Titan, 70 percent of sales)
Gross margin		$24,000	
Operating expenses:			Budget for the month
Selling expenses	$10,200		Experience (for Titan, $2,400 fixed
General expenses	4,000		costs plus variable costs of 2 percent
			of sales)
Total operating expenses		14,200	
Net income from operations		$9,800	
Other expense:			
Interest expense		500	Outstanding debt
Net profit before taxes		$9,300	
Income taxes		2,790	Tax rate of 30 percent
Net profit after taxes		$6,510	
Earnings withdrawn		5,000	Owner's intention
Retained earnings		$1,510	

[1] Not a real company.

Exhibit 14

Titan Manufacturing Company [1]

Projected Balance Sheet

December 31, 19___

		Figures based <u>on</u>:
Current assets:		
Cash	$40,000	Desired cash balance equal to 15 days' sales
Accounts receivable	80,000	Average collection period of 30 days' sales
Inventory	160,000	Monthly turnover of ¼ during this season
Total current assets	$280,000	
Fixed assets	500,000	Present figure adjusted for month's depreciation
Total assets	$780,000	

Liabilities

Current liabilities:

Notes payable	$69,000		Amount of borrowed funds needed to balance assets
Accounts payable	76,000		Expectation of 60 days' purchases on the books
Accrued liabilities	11,000		Same as preceding period
Total current liabilities	$156,000		
Long-term debt	70,000		Unchanged
Total liabilities		$226,000	

Equity

Paid-in capital	$350,000		Unchanged
Retained earnings	204,000		Present amount plus earnings to be retained in Dec.
Total equity		554,000	
Total liabilities and equity		$780,000	

Points to remember. Bear in mind two characteristics of projected financial statements. *First,* these statements can be built up in a number of ways. The best approach is to rely on whatever information is fairly easy to get together and enables you to make the most accurate estimates for the various accounts. *Second,* remember that these statements are based on estimates and assumptions. They provide only a rough sketch of what may happen.

If actual performance differs widely from the estimates at any point, however, the reason should be sought. Was the estimate unrealistic, or were there weaknesses in your company's performance at that point? Whichever proves to be the case, the trouble spot should be attended to.

Looking Still Further Ahead

You may find it hard to estimate capital requirements in the more distant future by developing projected cash budgets and financial statements. Business expectations 24 months ahead, for instance, may be too uncertain for detailed schedules to be pieced together.

In such cases, ask yourself this question: "Do I expect to do the same volume of business 2 years from now, or do I expect to do *x* percent more business?" When you have the answer to that question, you can make a rough estimate of your capital requirements for the period. Here's how.

Examine past financial statements to find the normal cash, inventory, accounts receivable, accounts payable, and short-term borrowing *per dollar of sales.* Then multiply these amounts by the dollar sales volume you expect to be doing in 2 years. Add to existing fixed assets any additions you expect to make during the 2 years.

You are now well on your way to constructing a rough projected balance sheet for that time. A concluding step is to subtract total estimated liabilities from total estimated assets. The difference is the projected equity account.

Now compare this account with your existing equity account. The difference between the two will have to be made up by retained earnings plus growth capital.

Chapter 5

THE DIFFERENT TYPES OF FINANCING

IN THIS CHAPTER we will discuss distinctions among the three different types of financing: (1) equity capital, (2) working capital, and (3) growth capital. This distinction is important since you must first know the exact nature of what it is you need in order to obtain adequate financing.

Equity capital is the cornerstone in the financial structure of any company. As suggested in chapter 2, equity is technically that part of the balance sheet which reflects ownership of the company. It also represents the total value of the business since all other financing amounts to some form of borrowing which must ultimately be repaid. When a lending officer asks the question "What do you have in the business?" he is asking about your equity. Equity capital is not generally obtainable from institutions—at least not during the early stages of business growth. By way of distinction, working capital and growth capital can be obtained in a number of ways. Both become necessary when equity capital has been used to the limit of its availability. The working capital and growth capital extend the effectiveness of equity by providing the leverage on investment present in the financial picture of most successful businesses.

Working capital needs arise as a result of the ongoing activities of the business. Funds are required to carry accounts receivable, to obtain inventories, and to meet payroll. It is to satisfy such needs that working capital is required. In most businesses the magnitude of these needs vary during the year and it is the varying use of more or less money to finance these requirements during the business cycle which most quickly indentifies this funding requirement as working capital.

Growth capital, although frequently grouped together with working capital, is different in that this funding source is not directly related to the cyclical aspects of the business. Instead, growth capital is usually involved when the business is expanding or being altered in some significant way. Usually the change in the business can be expected to result in higher levels of general profitability and cash flow, and it is because of this change that various types of growth capital can be arranged. Rather than looking for seasonal liquidity or reducing this type of borrowing as in the case of working capital, lenders which make growth capital available frequently depend on increased profits to provide orderly repayment of such loans over a longer period of time.

The need for the presence of all three types of capital—equity capital, working capital, and growth capital—continues in every growing business. You should not expect a single financing program maintained for a short period of time to eliminate every future need.

As prospective suppliers of financing begin to analyze the requirements of your business, they will begin to distinguish among the three functional types of capital in the following way: (1) fluctuating (working capital), (2) amortizing (growth capital), and (3) permanent (equity capital).

If you are asking for a *working capital* loan, you will be expected to show how the loan can be reduced during your business's period of greatest liquidity during the business cycle or over a 1-year period. If you seek *growth capital,* you will be expected to show how these moneys will be used to make your business more profitable and generate extra cash which can be used to repay the loan over several years.

If, on the other hand, you are not asking for either working or growth capital, it is likely that a lender will say to you "we would like to be of assistance but we cannot invest in your business—this is the role of equity capital and we only make loans." This is a natural and quite logical response for a bank cannot be expected to become "locked in" with its money obtained from depositors as would a stockholder or a private investor whose moneys are placed at risk for dividend return or future capital gains.

With this background in mind, we can now begin to explore the various types of working capital loans and the sources which make this type of financing available to small businesses.

Chapter 6

UNSECURED BORROWINGS FOR WORKING CAPITAL

C HAPTER 3 DEFINED WORKING CAPITAL as the difference between current assets and current liabilities. To the extent that your working cash balances, cash accounts receivable, and inventories exceed trade credit—the gap must be financed. The simplest means of obtaining this working capital is by borrowing on an unsecured basis. Commercial banks are the largest source of this type of financing which has the following basic characteristics: (1) the loans are short term but renewable, (2) they fluctuate according to seasonal needs or follow a fixed schedule of reduction or amortization, (3) the loans call for periodical repayment, (4) they have no lien on any assets of the borrower, (5) they usually require that all indebtedness of the borrowing company to its principals be subordinated, (6) they have no priority over any common creditor of the borrower, and (7) they are granted primarily in ratio to the net current assets (working capital) position of the borrower.

Commercial banks usually prefer unsecured loans even though they do not include liens. This is because the loans are least costly to handle and administer. At the same time the banks grant unsecured credit only when they feel that the general liquidity and overall financial strength of your business relative to the size of the credit provide ample ability for repayment.

You may be able to predict that you require working capital financing for a specified interval, say 3 or 5 months, in which case the bank can issue a credit with that specific term. Most likely, however, your working capital need will continue over the cyclical growth pattern of your business. As suggested in the previous chapter, the usual function of working capital is to supplement the role of equity in connection with fluctuating needs over a period of the business cycle. Therefore, most unsecured credits are established on a year's basis and set up on the bank records as such. Despite the fact that a 1-year credit is established, the bank is likely to continue handling the transaction with a series of renewable 90-day notes. Theoretically, at 90-day intervals the bank will reappraise the credit situation and can conceivably call your note asking for repayment in full. In actual practice the bank is likely to feel that it has screened the credit sufficiently carefully in the beginning to review only once a year. Therefore, the 90-day maturity date is only a technicality; however, you must handle it properly by paying it off in cash on or before due date or, usually, "paying by renewal."

Although most unsecured loans fall into the category just described—that is, the 1-year line of credit consisting of a series of renewable 90-day notes—there is another type of working capital loan which is also frequently used. This is the amortizing loan which calls for a fixed program of reduction usually on a monthly or quarterly basis. If you borrow for working capital purposes on a amortizing basis, your bank is likely to agree to terms longer than a year so long as you comply with the schedule of stipulated principal reductions.

There is an important feature to the types of borrowing arrangements described above. Namely, while a loan commitment from a bank for working capital can only be negotiated for a relatively short term, after satisfactory performance during that term the arrangement can be continued indefinitely on the assumption that a good business relationship exists between you and your bank and that your creditworthiness has not been impaired.

"The Annual Clean-Up"

Once a year the bank will expect you to pay off your unsecured borrowings for perhaps 30 or 60 days and this is what is known as *"the annual clean-up."* This clean-up occurs during the period of greatest liquidity during the year when it is possible for your indebtedness to be at its lowest level. This normally occurs following a seasonal sales peak when inventories have been reduced and receivables are largely collected from customers prior to the beginning of a new business buildup.

You may discover that it becomes progressively more difficult to repay debt or "clean-up" and this condition usually occurs due to the following reasons: (1) your business is growing to the extent that this year's period of least activity represents a considerable increase over the corresponding period of the previous year, (2) you are increasing your immediate short-term capital requirement because of some new promotional program or addition to operations, or (3) you are experiencing a reduction in profitability and cash flow which, hopefully, is temporary in nature.

Frequently, such a condition will justify a combination of both open line "self-liquidating" financing and the amortizing type of unsecured borrowing. For example, you might try to arrange a combination of perhaps $15,000 of open line credit to handle peak financial requirements during the business cycle and at the same time $20,000 of amortizing unsecured borrowings to be repaid at a rate of say $4,000 per quarter. In appraising such a request for combination of unsecured loans, your commercial banker, if he is on his toes, will insist on an explanation based on past experience and future projection for both: (1) how the $15,000 of open line credit will be self-liquidating during the year with ample room for the annual clean-up and (2) how, as a result of increased profits and resulting cash flows, you can be expected to meet the schedule of amortization on the $20,000 portion.

Since unsecured loans provide no prior claim or lien on assets to the lender, you have to provide ample assurances as to liquidity and to overall financial health to qualify for this type of financing. Credit acceptability is usually based on the following: (1) debt-to-worth ratio and (2) net current asset position. In many instances debt-to-worth ratios of 2 to 1 or even 3 to 1 are quite acceptable. Beyond that limit, however, other financing techniques may have to be used. With regard to your net current asset position, banks normally limit their unsecured open lines to 40 percent or 50 percent of working capital, sometimes going a little higher to allow for seasonal peaks. Still other banks in appraising the suitability of an unsecured line focus on the current ratio as a rough index of liquidity and for most types of businesses an acceptable current ratio is 1.5 to 1.

Putting Your Best Foot Forward

It is important to present your company's case persuasively to the bank if you are to succeed in obtaining unsecured credit lines. You should have a financial plan which contains a cash budget for the next 12 months as well as a pro forma balance sheet and income statement. You should be prepared to explain fully how these statements have been prepared and the underlying assumptions on which the figures are based. Obviously, these assumptions should be supportable. One final reminder. Many banks prefer that statements be prepared by an outside accountant and submitted on his stationery. Perhaps it is sometimes unjustified, but the outside accountant or financial advisor frequently has additional credibility as the result of his professional experience with financial matters and familiarity with many businesses. Only you can judge whether the assistance of an outsider will be useful in negotiations with your commercial banker.

Chapter 7

SECURED WORKING CAPITAL FINANCING

YOUR COMPANY MAY HAVE REACHED THE POINT where it is ineligible for additional unsecured borrowing arrangements with a commercial bank. This may be because your bank has reached its lending limit or takes the view that additional unsecured credit cannot be extended.

Under the circumstances it may be possible to arrange for your bank to participate with a commercial finance company in offering a secured credit which may result in a more advantageous interest rate than would be obtainable with a straightforward secured lending program.

The principal distinction between unsecured lending discussed in the previous chapter and secured borrowing is the existence of a lien—that is, a prior claim on specific assets given by the borrower to the lender. Under the Uniform Commercial Code which has been adopted by all 50 States, all classes of liens today are now lumped together under the term "security interests" which forms the basis for a security agreement. The presence of the lien means that common creditors and trade suppliers cannot look to the value of certain assets for repayment except subject to the claims of lienholding lenders.

Accounts Receivable Financing

The most common form of secured financing involves liens against accounts receivable. This type of financing is offered both by commercial banks and commercial finance companies. While distinctions are made by lenders among industry and individual firms, advances can usually be obtained amounting from 70 percent to 90 percent of outstanding quality receivables. Usually an "open limit" is established which permits the amount of financing to fluctuate as your receivable portfolio grows or declines.

Although the stated interest charge may be higher than for unsecured bank borrowings, the actual money cost differential between secured and unsecured borrowing may not be so high as it initially appears. This is due to the fact that secured borrowing costs are usually calculated based on actual cash used by the borrower on a daily basis and interest charges computed in this fashion may prove more moderate in comparison with unsecured borrowing costs which usually involve compensating balance requirements and other costs not included in the stated interest rates.

Factoring

As noted, accounts receivable financing involves borrowing with your accounts receivable as collateral. In factoring, unlike accounts receivable financing, the receivables are actually purchased by the factor without recourse. This non-recourse arrangement is normally limited, however, to the credit risk and the factor is protected against circumstances which would invalidate sales. Factoring is logical when it makes sense for outside parties to assume the responsibility for follow-up and collection. Traditionally, factors are used in industries where they have better firsthand knowledge of customers and their creditworthiness than do the sellers and where as a consequence, they can be more effective in converting the accounts receivable into cash.

Secured working capital financing can also be obtained by *pledging inventories*. In some instances inventories are stored in public warehouses where disinterested third parties having no affiliation with the borrower can provide protection for the associated lenders. A variation used by many companies for inventory financing involves field warehousing in which a clearly delineated area is set aside on the premises of the buyer enabling a distinterested third party to take full responsibility for the inventory against which credits are extended. Depending on the nature of your business and conditions in your industry, it may be possible to obtain a 60 percent to 75 percent advance with inventory as a lien.

Chapter 8

SECURED GROWTH
CAPITAL FINANCING

L ENDERS ASSUME THAT WORKING CAPITAL LOANS—whether extended on a secured or an unsecured basis—will be repaid through the automatic liquidation of receivables and inventories during the course of the business cycle. Thus, it is the inherent liquidity of the business rather than overall profitability which supports such borrowing programs. By the way of contrast growth capital loans are extended for longer periods of time and are repaid from profits rising from business activities extending several years into the future. It is logical, therefore, that growth capital loans are secured by collateral which remains unchanged in the possession of the borrower; that is, the noncurrent of fixed assets such as machinery and equipment.

In working capital financing primary credit emphasis is placed on the quality of collateral. For growth capital lending stress will be placed on underlying rationale for the borrowing. In other words, you will need to demonstrate that growth capital can be used to increase cash flows or sources of payment through increased sales, cost savings, or greater production efficiencies. Although your building, equipment, or machinery will probably be the collateral for growth capital borrowing, the use of the funds is not necessarily restricted to purchase of additional equipment. Any general business purpose is eligible so long as it promises possibilities of success.

Although you may wish to borrow to acquire a specific piece of new equipment if substantial amounts of growth capital are involved, the lender is likely to insist that all machinery and equipment of the business be pledged and the percentage of the advance is likely to range somewhere between 25 percent and 75 percent of the equipments' book value.

Leasing

For a particular piece of new equipment it may be possible to arrange a lease in which case you will not actually own the equipment but, rather, enter into an arrangement where your firm obtains exclusive use of it over a specified number of years. Such an arrangement may have possible tax advantages besides releasing funds which would otherwise be tied up in ownership of the equipment.

Conditional Sales Purchases

Still another variation involves purchasing equipment on a time payment basis. Naturally, the ownership of the property under such an arrangement is retained by the seller until the buyer has made all the required monthly or quarterly payments over the term of the contract.

Sale Leasebacks

Most purchased leases involve new equipment. It is sometimes possible to sell equipment which your business owns to a leasing company and then lease it back. It may be possible under such an arrangement to obtain an advance equal to or larger than what could be obtained through a conventional mortgage financing arrangement.

Pulling the Various Elements Together

Many business situations are best financed by a combination of the various types of credit arrangements described earlier. For example, your business may qualify for secured bank credit extended on a regular 90-day renewable basis so long as it is possible to "clean-up" or "rest" the line annually. If the short-term, self-liquidating facet of your financial requirement is separated from the longer-term components, this may indeed be possible. The longer-term components are more likely to be accommodated by some form or combination of types of secured financing. Receivables financing and warehouse lending may be possibilities and these, in turn, may be supplemented by chattel mortgage borrowings or one of the other forms of borrowing against fixed assets. Commercial finance companies are well qualified to help you develop a proper solution in the use of secured financing options together with unsecured borrowings.

Chapter 9

THE SMALL BUSINESS ADMINISTRATION

THE SMALL BUSINESS ADMINISTRATION (SBA) is an independent agency of the Federal Government, established by Congress to advise and help the Nation's small businesses. Its four major areas of activity are:

- Helping small companies find adequate capital and credit.
- Providing management, financial, and production counsel.
- Licensing and regulating small business investment companies.
- Helping small business get a fair share of Government procurement contracts and surplus sales.

Financial Counseling

If you need counseling in connection with financing your business, you may get help from financial specialists assigned to SBA's field offices, which are listed on the inside back cover of this booklet. These specialists are prepared to advise you on a wide range of financial problems. They may be able to help you get a loan on reasonable terms from a bank or other private source. Or they may be able to show you how to solve your problem without borrowing—by making some changes in your management or financial policies or methods.

51

SBA Loans

If borrowing does appear to be necessary or advisable, and if no private source can be found, SBA will consider making the loan. However, by law, SBA cannot consider a loan application unless there is evidence that the loan could not be obtained elsewhere on reasonable terms. This usually means a letter from one or two banks notifying you that your application for a loan has been rejected and the reasons why they are unable to assist.

It is the policy of SBA to encourage loans by banks and other private institutions. Therefore, if the bank is willing to supply part but not all of the funds needed, SBA will consider participating with it in a loan to the businessman or guaranteeing part of a loan made to him by the bank. SBA may either provide or guarantee up to 90 percent of a bank loan or $350,000, whichever is less.

If the bank cannot extend credit even in participation with SBA, the borrower may apply for a "direct" SBA loan—that is, a loan for which SBA supplies all the funds. Under the law, SBA cannot enter into a direct-loan agreement if a participation loan is available, nor into an immediate participation agreement if a loan is available on the guaranty basis.

The key features of SBA's principal business loan programs are shown in exhibit 15. Lower interest rates, longer maturities, and more liberal collateral requirements than those shown are granted when substantial economic injury has been suffered through (1) a major natural disaster as determined by the President or the Secretary of Agriculture; (2) a small firm's inability to process or market a product for human consumption because of disease or toxicity of the product; or (3) relocation of a small firm as a result of its displacement by a federally aided urban-renewal, highway, or other construction program.

Are you eligible for an SBA loan? To be eligible for consideration for a business loan from the Small Business Administration, a company must qualify as a small business and must meet SBA's credit requirements.

For business loan purposes, SBA defines a small business as one that (1) is independently owned and operated, (2) is not dominant in its field, and (3) meets certain standards of size in terms of employment or annual receipts. These standards vary for different types of businesses. Call or write the nearest SBA field office for the specific standards for your industry.

In addition to qualifying as a small business, a loan applicant must meet the following general credit requirements:

● The applicant must be of good character.

● There must be evidence that he has the ability to operate his business successfully.

● He must have enough capital in the business so that, with the loan assistance from SBA, he will be able to operate on a sound financial basis.

● The past record and future prospects of the business must indicate ability to repay the loan out of income from the business.

Since the Small Business Administration is a public agency using taxpayers' funds, it has an unusual responsibility as a lender. Therefore, it will not make loans to a few types of businesses nor for certain purposes. For example, loans will not be made to gambling enterprises nor for the purpose of speculation in real or personal property.

What to do. If you have been unable to obtain funds elsewhere and intend to apply for an SBA loan, you should first visit the nearest SBA field office (see inside back cover) and discuss your situation with an SBA financial specialist. This is not a rigid requirement, but it will be well worth your while. You will find his advice most valuable in the preparation of your loan application, and probably even beyond that.

Take with you the business records you prepared in connection with your application for a bank loan and any other information that might help the financial specialist understand your problems. No charge is made for information and counsel furnished by SBA either in connection with the preparation and filing of an application or as part of its general counseling program.

Your banker can probably supply the application forms you need. If not, you can get them from the SBA field office.

State and Local Development Companies

The Small Business Administration is also authorized to lend funds to State and local development companies for use in financing specific small businesses. An increasing number of State and local communities are organizing development corporations, or industrial foundations, to promote the establishment or expansion of businesses in their areas. Services offered by these organizations may include the following:

Exhibit 15   Key Features of SBA's Small Business Loan Programs

	BUSINESS LOANS * Direct, Immediate Participation and Guaranty Loans	ECONOMIC OPPORTUNITY LOANS * Direct, Immediate Participation and Guaranty Loans
WHO IS ELIGIBLE?	Most businesses that are: (1) independently owned and operated and not dominant in their fields; (2) unable to obtain private financing on reasonable terms; (3) not eligible for financing from other government agencies; (4) qualified as "small" under SBA's size standards, based on dollar volume of business or number of employees.	Low income or disadvantaged persons who have lacked the opportunity to start or strengthen a small business and cannot obtain the necessary financing from other sources on reasonable terms.
LOAN PURPOSES	Business construction, conversion or expansion, purchase of equipment, facilities, machinery, supplies or materials and working capital.	Any use which will carry out the purposes shown above; generally, the same as other business loans.
MAXIMUM AMOUNT	$350,000**to any one borrower. This is the maximum SBA share of an immediate participation loan, where SBA and private lending institution each put up part of loan funds immediately; or a guaranteed loan, made jointly by SBA and a private lending institution and maximum SBA direct loan, one made entirely by the Agency.	$50,000 to any one borrower, as SBA share of loan.

INTEREST RATE	Maximum 5½% per annum on direct loan and SBA share of an immediate participation loan. However, If participating institution sets a lower rate, SBA will match this rate to a minimum of 5% on its share. On the bank's share of an immediate participation loan, the lending institution may set reasonable and legal rate with a maximum ceiling set by SBA from time to time. On a guaranty loan, bank may set legal and reasonable rate, with a maximum ceiling set by SBA from time to time. If SBA purchases its share, rate on this share is 5½%.	On direct loans and SBA share of immediate participation loans, the rate is set periodically, based on a statutory formula. Bank rate same as on other business loans.
MATURITY	Maximum of 10 years as a rule. However, working capital loans generally are limited to 6 years, while portions of loans for construction may have maximum of 15 years.	Maximum of 15 years. Working capital loans generally limited to a 10-year maximum.
TYPE OF COLLATERAL	Real estate or chattel mortgage; assignment of warehouse receipts for marketable merchandise; assignment of certain types of contracts; guarantees or personal endorsements; in some instances assignment of current receivables.	Any worthwhile collateral which is available or will be acquired with the proceeds of the loan.

* Under the Handicapped Assistance Loan Program, financial aid is available to handicapped individuals to start or operate small firms, and to nonprofit organizations which employ the handicapped to make a product or provide a service. Further details at local SBA office.

** At times, SBA may have lower ceilings in order to conserve limited funds.

● *Buying, developing, and selling industrial sites.* This usually results in less delay and more reasonable prices for the small manufacturer seeking a site than negotiations through regular business channels.

● *Buying and building plants for lease or sale.* Here, too, a purchase price may be lower than would have to be paid otherwise. If the plant is leased, less investment in fixed assets will be necessary, with more money available for working capital.

● *Providing funds by direct intermediate—or long-term loans or by purchase of stock in the business.* In some cases, development companies will lend larger amounts in proportion to the value of the security and for longer periods than is customary for banks.

● *Giving management, engineering, and other counseling services to small businesses.* By pooling the knowledge of the businessmen of the community, an industrial foundation is often able to provide expert advice.

The primary purpose of development companies is to promote the economic welfare of their communities. Therefore, the small businessman who seeks their cooperation needs to be able to show that substantial benefit to the community will result.

Small Business Investment Companies

Small business investment companies (SBIC's) may make long-term loans to incorporated and unincorporated small businesses to provide funds for sound financing, growth, modernization, and expansion. Except under special circumstances, these loans must have final maturities of not less than 5 years and not more than 20 years. Since a major function of SBIC's is to provide equity financing for small businesses, they are discussed more fully in the next chapter.

Chapter 10

SBIC'S AND OTHER SOURCES OF VENTURE CAPITAL

S MALL BUSINESS INVESTMENT COMPANIES (SBIC'S) are licensed and financed by the Small Business Administration (SBA) for the purpose of providing venture capital to small business concerns. This capital may be in the form of secured and/or unsecured loans, debt securities with equity characteristics, or "pure" equity securities which are represented by common and preferred stock.

Venture capital is extremely difficult to define; however, it is characterized as being high risk with the principal objective of capital gains. The structure and terms of the financing are responsive to the needs of the small business rather than to the requirements of the venture investors. Additionally, and probably more importantly, venture capital is characterized by a continuing active relationship between the small business and the venture capitalist.

At the present time, there are about 300 SBIC's with total capital resources of $875 million which includes both private and Government capital. These SBIC's have a portfolio of approximately 5,000 small businesses with active financing balances of over $500 million.

The SBIC's are able to borrow $3 for every $1 of private capital through a line of credit which has been estabilshed by SBA for SBIC's with the Federal Financing Bank. Ample funds are available for eligible SBIC's on a monthly basis.

Section 301 (d) SBIC's (MESBIC's)

Minority enterprise SBIC's (MESBIC's) have been formed for the purpose of providing venture capital and equity financing to small businesses owned by persons who are socially or economically disadvantaged. Usually included in this clientele group are Blacks, Puerto Ricans, Mexican-Americans, Indians, and Eskimos.

MESBIC's have a certain structure similar to SBIC's except that the nature of SBA leverage is different. Certain rules and regulations of SBA have been liberalized to enable MESBIC's to overcome certain financing problems unique to businesses owned by members of minority groups. Frequently, MESBIC's invest in tandem with commercial banks with funds 90 percent guaranteed under other SBA programs.

Today, there are about 80 MESBIC's with total capital resources of $75 million. MESBIC's have a portfolio consisting of over 1,100 small minority firms.

Venture Capital

In addition to SBIC's and MESBIC's, there are two other types of venture capital companies which provide venture and equity financing to small businesses.

First are the *private venture capital firms*. These firms consist primarily of professional partnerships and corporations which are backed by institutional investors such as insurance companies, bank trust departments, wealthy families and others .

Second, there are *family venture capital firms* which represent some of the country's wealthiest families. While again there are differences in practices among family venture capital firms, these enterprises are typically more willing to invest in early stage investments, particularly in small businesses whose products or services are expected to have a major impact or social effect on our society.

When to Turn to Venture Capitalists

If your business requires additional equity capital and if internally available moneys are simply inadequate, some form of venture capital participation may make sense. Venture capitalists will expect a relatively high percentage of ownership in your company for a given amount of money initially invested in the business. At the same time these financiers may provide invaluable assistance in lining up additional outside financing, marketing and product ideas, and general management consulting.

It is important for you to recognize that you are taking on a partner who will maintain an active interest in your business and its direction when you become involved with venture capitalists. They can provide guidance and open many doors, and they are generally patient and sympathetic to the problems associated with building a small business. They are usually prepared to wait longer than the average investor for profits to arrive so long as you are conscientiously pursuing your objectives. Most venture capitalists expect a 15 percent rate of return on their investment or higher and expect to see profits within a five to seven year period.

Chapter 11

FOR FURTHER INFORMATION

THIS BOOKLET HAS DESCRIBED several concepts and tools of financial analysis that can help the small business owner-manager interpret financial data and manage the operations of his businesss. But it is important to remember that understanding and applying these tools successfully requires more than a knowledge of how the tools work. It is also essential to understand when the tools should be used and, more important, what their strengths and limitations are.

Financial analysis cannot be carried out in a routine, standardized way. You must be able to tailor the concepts and tools to the specific requirements of your business. You must ask yourself, "What questions need to be asked about my business?" and then, "What approach shall I use to get practical answers to these questions?"

Before analyzing a financial problem, ask yourself these questions:

"What factors, trends, relations, and time periods have a bearing on the problem?"

"What tool or method of analysis will be most useful?"

"How much detail work is justified?"

The amount of literature in the field of business finance is vast. Some of the information is not applicable to the finance problems of small businesses. Much of it is, however, and some of it is designed especially for small business.

The following lists may be useful to small business owner-managers who wish to study the subject of business finance further. The lists are necessarily brief. No slight is intended toward authors and sources not included.

60

Sources of Industry Ratio Data

Among the best known sources of industry ratio data with which to compare your own ratios are the following:

Key Business Ratios. Published annually by Dun and Bradstreet, Inc., 99 Church St., New York, NY 10007.

Covers 125 lines of business activity, including manufacturing, wholesaling, retailing, and construction industries.

Statement Studies. Published annually by Robert Morris Associates, National Association of Bank Loan Officers and Credit Men, Philadelphia National Bank Building, Philadelphia, PA 19107.

Based on data collected from member banks of the association. Covers approximately 300 lines of business.

Barometer of Small Business. Published semi-annually by the Accounting Corporation of America, 1929 First Ave., San Diego, CA 92101.

The businesses covered here are mostly retail and commercial service groups.

Specialized Industry Reports. There are many sources of ratio data specializing in single industries or industry groups. These sources include trade associations, specialized accounting firms, trade magazines, universities, some large industrial corporations, and several Government agencies. A number of them are listed in the booklet *Ratio Analysis for Small Business* (see below, under "U.S. Government Publications"). This booklet also has more detailed information about the publications whose specific titles are mentioned above.

U.S. Government Publications

● The following publications may be purchased from the Superintendent of Documents, Washington, D.C. 20402. Write for current price and availability.

Cost Accounting for Small Manufacturers (SBMS No. 9). Small Business Administration.

Ratio Analysis for Small Business (SBMS No. 20). Small Business Administration.

Guides for Profit Planning (SBMS No. 25). Small Business Administration.

Financial Control by Time-Absorption Analysis (SBMS No. 37). Small Business Administration.

Buying and Selling a Small Business (Nonseries). Small Business Administration.

The following publications are available free from your nearest Small Business Administration field office.

Management Aids for Small Manufacturers
    Financial Audits: A Tool for Better Management (MA 176).
    The ABC's of Borrowing (MA 170).
    Is Your Cash Supply Adequate (MA 174).
    Basic Budgets for Profit Planning (MA 220).

Small Marketers Aids
    Building Strong Relations with Your Bank (SMA 107).
    Controlling Cash in Small Retail and Service Firms (SMA 110).
    Budgeting in a Small Service Firm (SMA 146).

Books

Entrepreneurship and Venture Management. Clifford M. Baumback. 1975. Prentice-Hall, Inc., Englewood Cliffs, NJ 07632.

Guide to Buying or Selling a Business. James M. Hansen, 1975. Prentice-Hall, Inc., Englewood Cliffs, NJ 07632.

How to Run a Small Business. J. K. Lasser Tax Institute. 1974. McGraw-Hill Book Company, Inc., 1221 Avenue of the Americas, New York, NY 10020.

Small Business Management Fundamentals. Dan Steinhoff. 1974. McGraw-Hill Book Company, Inc., 1221 Avenue of the Americas, New York, NY 10020.

The Financing of Small Business. James Bates. 1971. Sweet & Maxwell, London, England.

Venture Capital: A Guidebook for New Enterprises. Boston College Management Institute, 1972. Superintendent of Documents, Washington, DC 20402.

Why, When and How to Go Public. G. Scott Hutchinson. 1970. Presidents Publishing House, Inc., 575 Madison Ave., New York, NY 10022.

Financing Minority Businesses. Robert Morris Associates, Philadelphia National Bank Building, Philadelphia, PA 19107.

How to Start Your Own Business. William D. Putt. 1974. MIT Press, 28 Carleton St., Cambridge, MA 02142.

Guide to Venture Capital Sources. Stanley M. Rubel. 1970. Capital Publishing Corp., 10 LaSalle St., Chicago, IL 60603.

Steps to Starting a Business. Brigid Brady. 1969. Bank of America, San Francisco, CA 94137.

Complete Guide to Financing Management for Small and Medium-Sized Companies. D. S. Brightly, *et al.* 1971. Prentice-Hall, Inc., Englewood Cliffs, NJ 07632.

Handbook for Manufacturing Entrepreneurs. Robert S. Morrison, Western Reserve Press, Inc., 3530 Warrensville Center Rd., Cleveland, OH 44122.

Periodicals

"The Art of Saying No." William R. Sears. *Nation's Business,* October 1974.

"Venture Management and the Small Businessman." Donald C. King and Robert L. Thornton. *Journal of Small Business Management,* October 1974.

"A Method of Investment Evaluation for Smaller Companies." Bernard Schwab and Helmut Schwab. *Management Services,* July–August 1969.

"Buy Your Company?" A. Weimer. *Iron Age,* June 21, 1973.

"Computer-Based Financial Management System for Small Business." H. Chen and R. C. Kick. *Management Advisor,* November 1973.

"Control Methods for Small Business." D. A. Reddington. *Management Accounting,* September 1973.

"How Smaller Companies are Tackling Their Financial Problems." B. Munder. *Management Review,* January 1975.

"Tax Considerations for Small Business." J. L. Rhoads. *Management Accounting,* January 1975.

"LIFO and Small Businesses." *Journal of Accounting,* April 1975.

"Branch Manager, Small Firm's Friend." G. Wood. *Banker,* August 1974.

"Financing Black Enterprise." T. Bates. *Journal of Finance,* June 1974.

"Designing an Accounting System for a Small Business." J. Brown. *Management Accounting,* June 1975.

"Small Business Financial Model." C. H. Chapman. *Management Accounting,* July 1975.